LYDIA LEE

THE WELL-DESIGNED ACCESSORY DWELLING UNIT

FITTING GREAT ARCHITECTURE INTO SMALL SPACES

SCHIFFER PUBLISHING
4880 Lower Valley Road • Atglen, PA 19310

Other Schiffer Books by the Author:

Library of Congress Control Number: 2024931564

Edited by Jesse J. Marth

Designed by Molly Shields

Photo credits: Cover: Leonid Furmansky; Back Cover (*l to r*): Bruce Damonte, Alyssa Lee Photography, and Sally Schoolmaster; pp. 2–3: Mark Woods Photography; p. 4: Leonid Furmansky; p. 6 (*l to r*): Janis Nicolay, Abodu, and Mark Woods Photography; p. 8: Alyssa Lee Photography; p. 11: Bruce Damonte; p. 12: Janis Nicolay; p. 15 (*l to r*): Yoshihiro Makino, Cortez Media Group, and Leonid Furmansky; and p. 16: Bruce Damonte

Type set in Effra/Cambria

ISBN: 978-0-7643-6739-7

Printed in China

Published by Schiffer Publishing, Ltd.

4880 Lower Valley Road

Atglen, PA 19310

Phone: (610) 593-1777; Fax: (610) 593-2002

Email: info@schifferbooks.com

Web: www.schifferbooks.com

MIX
Paper | Supporting responsible forestry
FSC® C104723

DEDICATED TO CHERYL WEBER,
WHO HAD THE IDEA FOR THIS BOOK

GREAT GOOD FOOD
PERSIA

CONTENTS

FOREWORD

Long before ADUs got their acronym, they existed under other names. The accessory dwelling unit has a long, secret history in Los Angeles.

When the city was formally subdivided into lots for single-family houses in the 1940s, there was always also a variety of additional structures that were present on the same properties. They included garages with laundry facilities, pool houses, and artist studios. There were garages converted into "mother-in-law" homes—also known as granny flats, garden cottages, and other fun names—and even second and third rental houses. In L.A., there have been so many forms of dwellings alongside your standard home that they have become their own pop culture tropes. For instance, the hippie meditation yurt has appeared on TV shows from *Magnum P.I.* to *Curb Your Enthusiasm* to *Shrinking*. Having other people on a property provides a lot of opportunities for interaction and comedy, as well as community building—an advantage loved by sitcom writers, as well as architects and urbanists.

When I first moved to L.A. in the 1990s, studying architecture at SCI-Arc, I would see rental listings for guesthouses in desirable locations around town. They always sounded so alluring, but they were mostly illegal and often far from idyllic. Even if they weren't all that they were made out to be in the ads, it was very common to rent a "back house." They provided housing for students and adult children and served as office space. At the time, they were part of a mini real estate boom that made living and working in the city more affordable. L.A. is a city of renters, and this situation was widely embraced. How many design firms got their start in the back house?

Those were the early days. While the state of California legalized granny flats and garage apartments in 1982, it wasn't until 2016 that the state did away with local barriers, such as restrictions on renting, that made them widely popular. Since then, some 60,000 small dwellings, now known as ADUs, have been permitted across the state.

In California, we are trying all sorts of progressive ways to respond to the housing crisis, and the accessory dwelling unit has come out of the shadows to be embraced as a legal and architecturally fruitful way of adding housing to our cities. As the 1950s desire for suburban living has been replaced with the drive for more-communal living, this low-key urbanism encourages more interaction and redefines community building. We're remodeling our neighborhoods and preserving existing streetscapes, adding strategic backyard interventions to create a better model of housing density.

An ADU's creative potential stems from the unique context of the backyard, since no backyard is the same. By giving homeowners the opportunity to develop their own property, multifamily, multigenerational housing can grow organically within an existing community. The new rules, smaller scale, and proportionally lower budgets allow young design firms and property owners in California to explore new kinds of domestic architecture in a way that hasn't been seen since the post-WWII modernist movement.

Are the ADUs in this book so creative because they're a romantic element of landscape architecture, like a "folly" in the garden? Or is it because at that scale, people feel they can actually build their dream house with super-high ceilings, bright colors, or completely operable walls? It turns out a lot of us are very happy living in a more manageable microenvironment than we ever were in McMansions. Increasingly, it seems as if people are building their ideal small and efficient house, moving into it, and then renting out their bigger previous house as a way of keeping their property, paying their bills, and decreasing their carbon footprint.

This book takes us through some of the most creative ADUs and the possibilities right in your own backyard. As an architect, I find these tiny dwellings and the exuberant, blue-sky thinking they represent utterly contagious.

Barbara Bestor
Principal, Bestor Architecture

ACKNOWLEDGMENTS

I would like to thank all the architects who sent me information about their ADUs for consideration. For every ADU that made it into the book, there is a fantastic project that isn't quite finished yet. I can't wait to see how they all turn out. I am continually amazed by how much wonderful architecture you can fit into one small space.

I also want to thank my husband, Ed, for building a "bunny ADU" in the backyard while I was writing this book. It's a wooden box about three feet long and about a foot tall that is open at both ends, and it gives our two pet rabbits a place to hang out when it rains. In true ADU style, it is made out of plywood.

INTRODUCTION

ALL ABOUT ADUs

An ADU, which stands for "accessory dwelling unit," is essentially a small house that is on the same property as another house. It has all the functionality of a home, including a bathroom and a kitchen. But it isn't legally a house that can be sold separately, like a condo or duplex. These small homes are also referred to as in-law units, granny flats, casitas, and guesthouses. In Canada, they are called laneway houses, since they are often built next to a laneway, or alleyway.

Note that an ADU doesn't have to be a separate building. It can be a renovated space within an existing house (an internal or interior ADU), or an addition to a house (attached ADUs). ADUs that are separate are sometimes called "detached ADUs."

According to a Freddie Mac study, there were 1.4 million ADUs across the United States as of 2019, and their numbers have been increasing about 9 percent each year. The study notes that detached ADUs are more common in western metro areas, while in older East Coast cities, converted attics, basements, and garages are more prevalent.

People often build ADUs to host family and friends. For instance, an ADU can house an older family member who used to live independently, or serve as training wheels for a young person transitioning into independent living. Alternatively, they can provide extra living space, functioning as a home office or exercise studio. ADUs can also be rented out and bring in additional income as a long-term rental or home share. "The same unit can be used for multiple purposes over the course of its life," says David Morley, an urban planner at the American Planning Association in Chicago. "It's a pretty durable idea that has been with us for a long time."

At the start of the twentieth century, ADUs were commonplace in the United States. A home would have extra quarters inside the main building, and outbuildings of all sorts proliferated. After World War II, planning codes enforced zoning that specified one house per lot, defining the suburban landscape. Having another

residence on your property, no matter how small it was or whether it was tucked inside your house, was outlawed. But in areas where housing was in high demand, people built them anyway. By 1960, San Francisco had somewhere between 20,000 and 30,000 of these mostly illegal residences. In 2014, the city passed laws to help owners legalize an estimated 30,000 to 50,000 unpermitted ADUs, most of which are converted garages or basements.

Today, many parts of the country are experiencing a severe housing crisis and especially lack affordable housing. To increase the number of housing units, some cities are encouraging ADUs by removing or reducing restrictions and expediting the permitting process. California, Oregon, Washington, and several other states have passed legislation that restrains their cities from blocking ADUs. "ADUs are a great start toward fixing the housing crisis," says Morley. "They're probably the gentlest way to add density since the street view is the same—there's no visual cue that a neighborhood is changing."

PLENTY

In addition to welcoming ADUs, cities and states are also considering broader zoning reforms. There is a growing trend toward eliminating single-family zoning and allowing more duplexes and triplexes to be built—which means that in those areas, you should be able to design an ADU that can be sold separately, or turn an existing ADU into a legally separate residence (sometimes referred to as "condoizing" an ADU). Check with your local jurisdiction about your current options, and what you can do to design an ADU for a potential split if that is of interest.

GETTING STARTED

Your first step is to check whether your city allows the construction of an ADU on your property, which is likely zoned for a single-family house. The fastest way to figure this out may be to call your planning department; they can look up your address and tell you about any obvious obstacles, such as a utility easement that would prevent any construction over it.

If you are fortunate to live in an ADU-friendly jurisdiction, size and budget are your limiting factors. "The basic questions are "Do you have the space for it?' and "Can you afford it?" says Martina Davis, a planner who works for the city of San Jose, California. By looking up some ADU floor plans online, you can determine whether your backyard is big enough for a detached ADU. Be sure to factor in your city's requirements for "setbacks," or the minimum distance that the ADU must be from your property lines (back, front, and sides). There will also likely be limits on ADU height, square footage, and floor-to-area ratio (FAR, or square footage in relation to lot size).

To get a rough idea of what it will cost to build your ADU, find out what the cost per square foot for building a new home is in your area. Note that construction costs vary considerably from place to place. Keep in mind that since a detached ADU is essentially a small house, the cost per square foot will be greater than that of a standard-sized house. Once you calculate the construction cost, you'll need to add 15 to 20 percent to the total for "soft costs" such as architectural fees and permitting fees. If your city offers preapproved ADU plans, you may be able to save some on soft costs. An architect or builder will be able to tell you whether your estimate is in the right ballpark. And it's wise to include a budget for landscape design. Whether you envision the ADU as an extension of your house or a totally separate entity, the outdoor spaces are critical to defining that relationship. A rough estimate for landscape costs is 10 percent of the ADU construction cost.

"People should be prepared for sticker shock," says Ira Belgrade, the founder of YimbyLA, a Los Angeles–based company that builds ADUs. "In California, the state's ADU regulations overrode zoning codes, but they didn't override building codes. The biggest misconception is that people think it's easy to permit an ADU that's unpermitted or that it's somehow less expensive to build one, now that we have state laws in place. But it's expensive to build to code."

On the positive side, depending on where you live, you may be able to tap into a well-developed ADU industry and many professionals and companies with ADU experience. You can work with an architect or designer to build a custom ADU, or you may also have the option of purchasing a prefabricated ADU that arrives nearly complete on your site.

FINANCING YOUR ADU

To pay for the construction of an ADU, there are numerous financing strategies, including pooling resources with family members. Financing options can get complicated, so it's a good idea to consult a professional.

Assuming you have some equity in your current home, you have various ways to borrow against it. One popular way to finance an ADU is to take out a home equity line of credit (HELOC), which provides a lot of flexibility since borrowers can decide when and how much they want to borrow, rather than borrowing a lump sum. However, HELOCs usually have variable interest rates, which means that your interest payments may be higher than other financing options.

If you're considering an ADU purely as an investment, the general rule of thumb is that the monthly rent of your investment should be at least 1 percent of the purchase price (in this case, the amount you spend building the ADU). "The 1 percent rule is a very broad way to help you determine whether it will pencil out," says Stewart Hulick, a broker in Portland who has built three ADUs. To get a better idea of whether the anticipated rent will cover the costs, total up the principal plus interest on your loan, the increase in your property taxes, and the increase in your homeowner's insurance, then use that sum to calculate your monthly costs.

PROFESSIONAL ADVICE

"Building an ADU is very similar to building a whole new house, and in some cases more difficult since every square foot is valuable. An ADU can be an addition, an age-in-place apartment, a studio, or even an income earner; consider the big picture when figuring out a budget." —Geoffrey Warner, Alchemy Architects, St. Paul, Minnesota

"Hire an architect. It's a small space. Design it right and it will be so much more enjoyable!" —Bo Sundius, Bunch Design, Los Angeles

"ADUs tend to be more expensive per square foot, and building anything takes longer than most people realize. Expectations about time—'It's small; it will be fast!'—or budget—'It's small; it will be cheap!'—are likely to be dashed. It may take awhile for you to come to terms with the budget and schedule." —Andrew Atwood, First Office, Los Angeles

"Make lists of 'must-haves' and 'nice-to-haves,' since it is hard to accomplish every need in such small projects. Balancing these two categories will hopefully yield a better end result." —Kailin Gregga, Best Practice Architecture, Seattle, Washington

"Try to eliminate hallways and consider using spiral stairs to save space across multiple levels. Think about furniture, even in the early design phase, to make sure your plan is as efficient as it can be—you might make room for much-needed storage, a patio, or extra outdoor space." —James Guillou, ORA, Los Angeles

"Don't have one big open room. There is no privacy if you have more than one occupant, and the perimeter, where you need windows for light and views, will be taken up with infrastructure and storage. Creating separate spaces gives you the opportunity to create different experiences." —Rudabeh Pakravan, Sidell Pakravan Architects, Berkeley, California

"Just do it! It's about adding value and future flexibility. It allows family structures to stay intact as they grow, age in place, and change and evolve over time on the same heritage property." —Andrew Dunbar, INTERSTICE Architects, San Francisco

"Consider site planning and landscaping carefully to optimize private access and outdoor space for both the ADU and the primary residence." —Dustin Stephens, Mobile Office Architects, Seattle

"Design for the future—think 20 to 30 years down the line. Sustainability features are worth it in the long run." —Prentis Hale, SHED Architecture & Design, Seattle

"Do something interesting that is also functional. And build the ADU that you would want to keep for the rest of your life." —Ben Warwas, Byben, Los Angeles

RECLAIMING THE BACKYARD

After adding an ADU, a Los Angeles backyard appears to increase in size.

PHOTOS COURTESY OF YOSHIHIRO MAKINO

Pastor and his son, Pastor Lee, enjoy their reconfigured backyard. The trellis-covered patio serves as an outdoor dining room, but it is technically a carport. Since the couple demolished their garage, the city required that they create two covered parking spaces.

The studio's walls are finished in plywood, and the vaulted ceiling is lined with white drywall to accentuate its height.

Returning home from a business trip, Gennifer was pretty sure that she had come down with COVID-19 after colleagues reported testing positive. "I didn't even come into the house; I just rolled my suitcase straight down the path into the ADU," she said. "It was great because I could see my family and I knew I was home and safe, but there was a guarantee that I wouldn't transfer it to them."

While the 465-square-foot studio has come in handy for quarantining and working from home during the pandemic, Gennifer and her husband, Pastor, built the ADU primarily as a guesthouse for their relatives visiting from out of state. Their home, a two-bedroom bungalow in L.A.'s Atwater Village neighborhood, couldn't readily accommodate their elderly parents, especially after the arrival of their second child. The couple, both of whom work in the TV and film industry, also wanted a home office space.

Originally, they contemplated renovating the home's detached one-car garage into a guest cottage. They consulted architect Rebecca Rudolph at Design, Bitches (DB). Evaluating the flimsy garage, which was only 5 feet from the house, Rudolph knew that the couple could gain a lot more for their renovation dollar by starting afresh.

As it turns out, the architects had completed a similar project just down the street, where they tore down an old garage and built a new guesthouse in the backyard. "In a lot of houses, there is a dead space in the back that nobody goes into," says Rudolph. "Placing the ADU at the back of the yard lets you fully use all of that space." She took the couple to see the "Garden House" project. It provided a vision for how much better their place could be. "When we walked

into it, I said, 'Well, this yard is way bigger than ours,'" says Gennifer. "But our lot was actually bigger than theirs. I said, 'I'm sold!'" Says Pastor, "It was a real lightbulb moment for us."

The studio is designed as an extension of the main house. Its living/dining space faces the house's dining room, and the new outdoor spaces are shared between the two. The couple decided to install a small pool for the kids while the backyard was in flux, and the ADU's bathroom has an exterior door for easy access from the pool. The architects finished the interior walls with marine-grade plywood and used the concrete slab foundation as the flooring. They also designed it for aging in place, with wide openings and flush thresholds. Both the main house and the ADU are painted the same shade of inky blue to tie the two buildings together visually; the architects have dubbed this project the "Midnight Room."

"The intent was to have the ADU be very simple and affordable and create a space that felt like a sanctuary and had its own personality," says Rudolph. "We also thought about it as a series of rooms that were very connected to the yard—it's a much bigger space than just the building itself."

A deep roof overhang and a boardwalk outside that lets water drain away makes it easier to create a flush threshold for the big sliding door. A thin mirrored panel to the right of the kitchen area makes the space appear bigger than it is.

The ADU is set up for an induction cooktop and a small refrigerator under the sink.

Exposed ceiling beams create interest overhead. Mori sconces from Rich Brilliant Willing, inspired by paper lanterns, produce a soft glow.

TACOPEDIA
The Taco Encyclopedia
REYNOLD BROWN

EXTRA STORAGE

After taking down the old garage, Pastor and Gennifer still needed a place to stow all their stuff. Rudolph designed two small rooms, about 50 square feet in total, which are part of the ADU but are accessible only from the outside. The first room has sliding doors for easy access and holds an extra fridge for overflow and outdoor dining. It also holds the family's bike rack, surfboards, and yard toys. The second room, which has folding fiberglass doors that are painted to match the exterior, is for Pastor's woodworking tools; he likes to wheel his tool cart onto the patio to work on projects.

NOTE: These rooms are not visible in the photographs but are visible in the plans.

The ADU's built-in wardrobe was custom designed by the architects and fabricated from Baltic birch plywood by local studio Waka Waka.

Inexpensive white tile is slightly offset to create an interesting pattern along the shower walls. A door leading outside allows the bathroom to be easily accessed from the pool.

In the bathroom, the architects integrated the clerestory window with the medicine cabinet, backsplash, and IKEA vanity, adding style without adding cost. The bathroom door has a standard door frame but was constructed carefully to be able to omit the door trim and still look refined.

The boardwalks that run in front of the ADU and connect it to the main house are inspired by *engawa*, the boardwalks that encircle traditional Japanese homes. They create a level path on the uneven site and strengthen the connection between the two buildings.

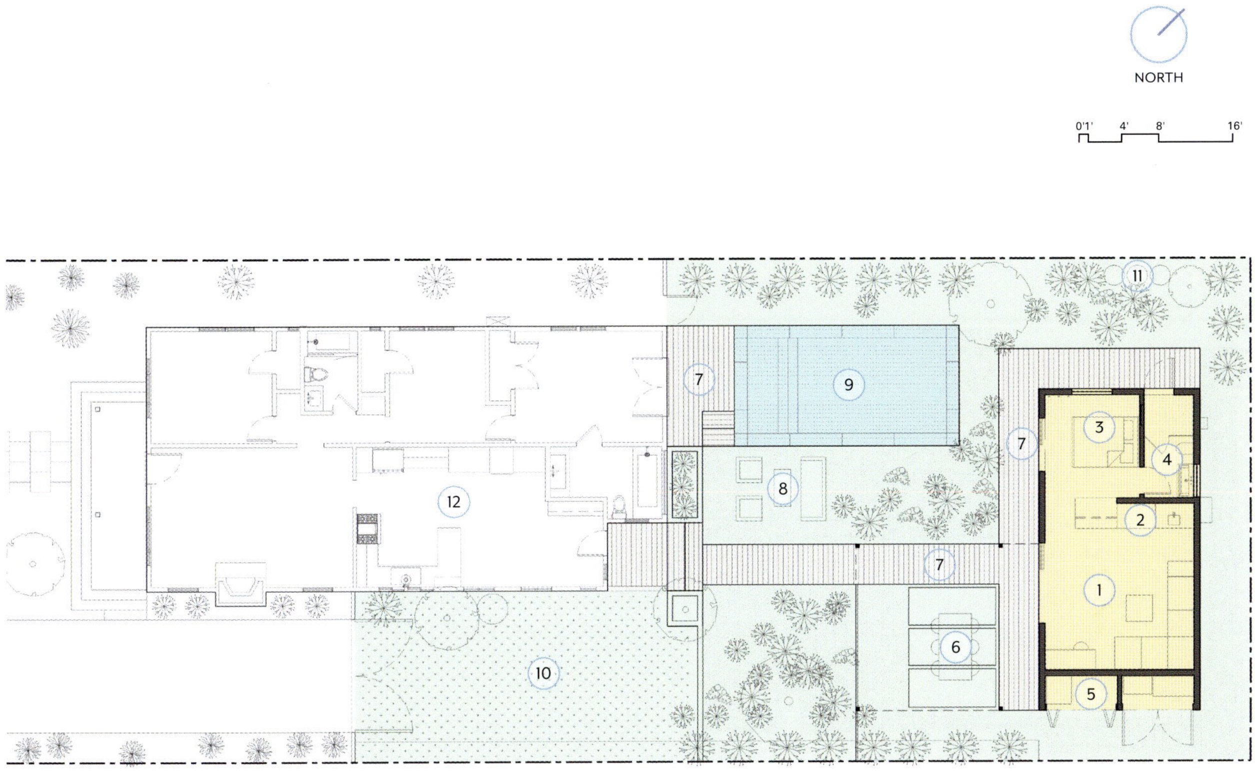

1. Living/Working Space
2. Kitchenette
3. Sleeping Area
4. Bathroom
5. Storage
6. Covered Dining
7. Decks/Walkways
8. Fire Pit
9. Swimming Pool
10. Drought-Tolerant Planting
11. Rain Barrels
12. Existing House

TOGETHER BUT SEPARATE

Two brothers in Austin, Texas, create an ADU designed to give each of them some privacy.

PHOTOS COURTESY OF LEONID FURMANSKY

Embellished with a chevron pattern, the ADU is interesting to look at from the main house. The patio off the ground-floor bedroom can also be accessed from the kitchen.

The knotty cedar paneling repeats on the inside. The kitchen island doubles as a dining table, with seating along the left side; it also has cabinets for additional storage.

A few years after graduating from college, Eric and his older brother, Patrick, decided to pool their resources and buy a three-bedroom house in Austin's East Side. Eric, who is in technology sales, and Patrick, who is a businessperson, had grown up in the city and wanted to continue living here. They figured that they could live in the home while continuing to make improvements to their investment. They decided to rent out part of the house and build an ADU to bring in additional rental income.

Their architect, Davey McEathron, had already steered the brothers clear of purchasing other properties that had unpermitted ADUs and additions that would have required them to make costly upgrades. The house, in the city's Holly neighborhood, had a big yard that backed up to an alleyway, making it a prime candidate for an ADU. The brothers took out a home mortgage as well as an additional loan for the ADU construction that was refinanced into the mortgage upon completion. McEathron's firm began designing an ADU that would add as much square footage as possible, with two bedrooms and two baths.

Because the city restricted the amount of impervious surface on the property, the 1,000-square-foot ADU had to be two stories tall.

Built-ins under the stairwell make the most of the ADU's limited square footage.

"We designed it as if we were moving into it," says Eric. "One thousand square feet is relatively small. Knowing that we were going to come into conflict and that we would potentially live there together as young adults, we wanted it to feel big and open but also be isolated from each other." The design team placed one bedroom downstairs and located the other bedroom upstairs on the opposite end of the house. To make it feel as big as possible, the architects designed vaulted ceilings on each floor and created three outdoor gathering spaces. In the years since the ADU was completed, both brothers have lived in the ADU, but never at the same time. They are on good terms, but they've also realized that they are happier living in separate dwellings.

While small, the ADU isn't lacking in architectural personality. Using relatively inexpensive knotty cedar panels, McEathron created an eye-catching chevron pattern on the gabled ends of the building. "The beauty of small projects like ADUs is that you can do some exciting moves without spending a lot of money—they beg to be dressed up," says McEathron. "My recommendation is that people should build something they really want to live in, and not build them just for financial reasons," says Eric.

The upstairs bedroom has its own private balcony.

Both bathrooms have showers. In retrospect, Eric would have installed a bathtub upstairs. "People like baths," he says.

A barn door made from reclaimed wood leads to the ground-floor bedroom.

WAR
AND PEACE

DEALING WITH SETBACKS

To meet city regulations, an ADU has to be built with minimum "setbacks" from the property lines.

When Eric and Patrick purchased the property in Austin, they didn't worry too much about the large pecan tree in the middle of the backyard. They figured they had room to maneuver since the ADU required only a 5-foot setback from the alleyway in back. McEathron's team submitted plans for an ADU that was about 6 feet from the alleyway and 13 feet away from the tree. However, their application was rejected because, as they found out later, the power lines in back were high-voltage transmission lines. To protect nearby properties in case a line came down in a storm, the power company required a 15-foot setback from the alleyway.

The architects dealt with this unexpected wrinkle and redid the plans so that the ADU was 15 feet from the alleyway and 4 feet from the pecan tree. To protect the tree's critical root zone, they cantilevered a section of the foundation. "It's a big, beautiful tree, and we definitely wanted to keep it," says McEathron.

The balcony of the upstairs bedroom creates the overhang of the front porch. "It's a clean and simple design, where you use the building to create a shape instead of sticking on an awning," notes McEathron.

On the side facing the alley, small windows bring in light. The ADU's standing-seam metal roof and fiber-cement siding are durable and low maintenance.

The ADU is closer to an existing pecan tree than anticipated, but the architects figured out how to preserve the tree.

Architect Davey McEathron relaxes on the roof deck.

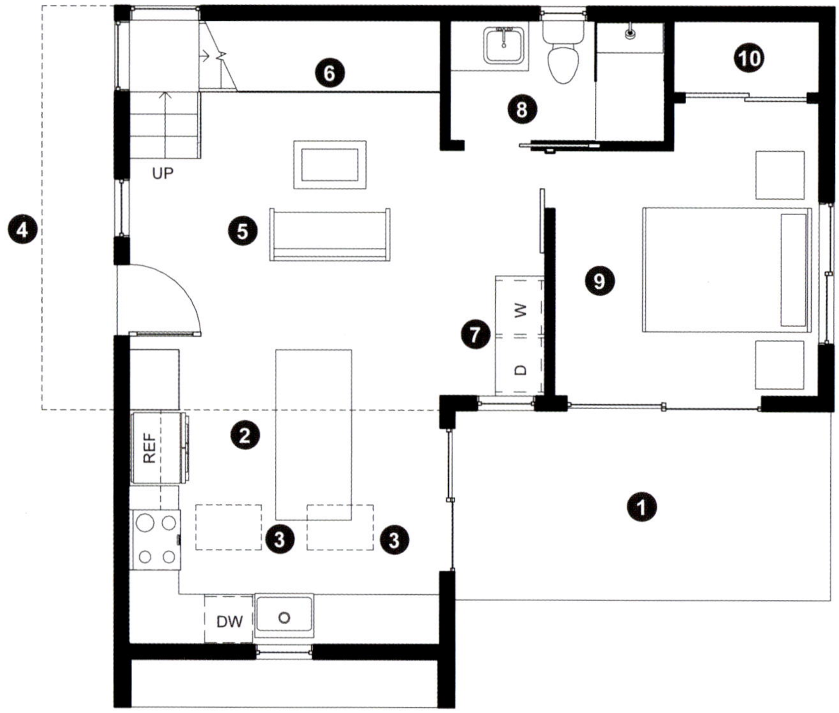

GROUND FLOOR

1. Patio
2. Vaulted Kitchen
3. Kitchen Skylights
4. Front Porch
5. Living
6. Under-Stair Built-In
7. Laundry Cabinet
8. Bath
9. Bedroom
10. Closet

SECOND FLOOR

1. Roof Deck
2. Bath
3. HVAC Closet
4. Closet
5. Bedroom
6. Private Roof Deck
7. Kitchen Roof Below

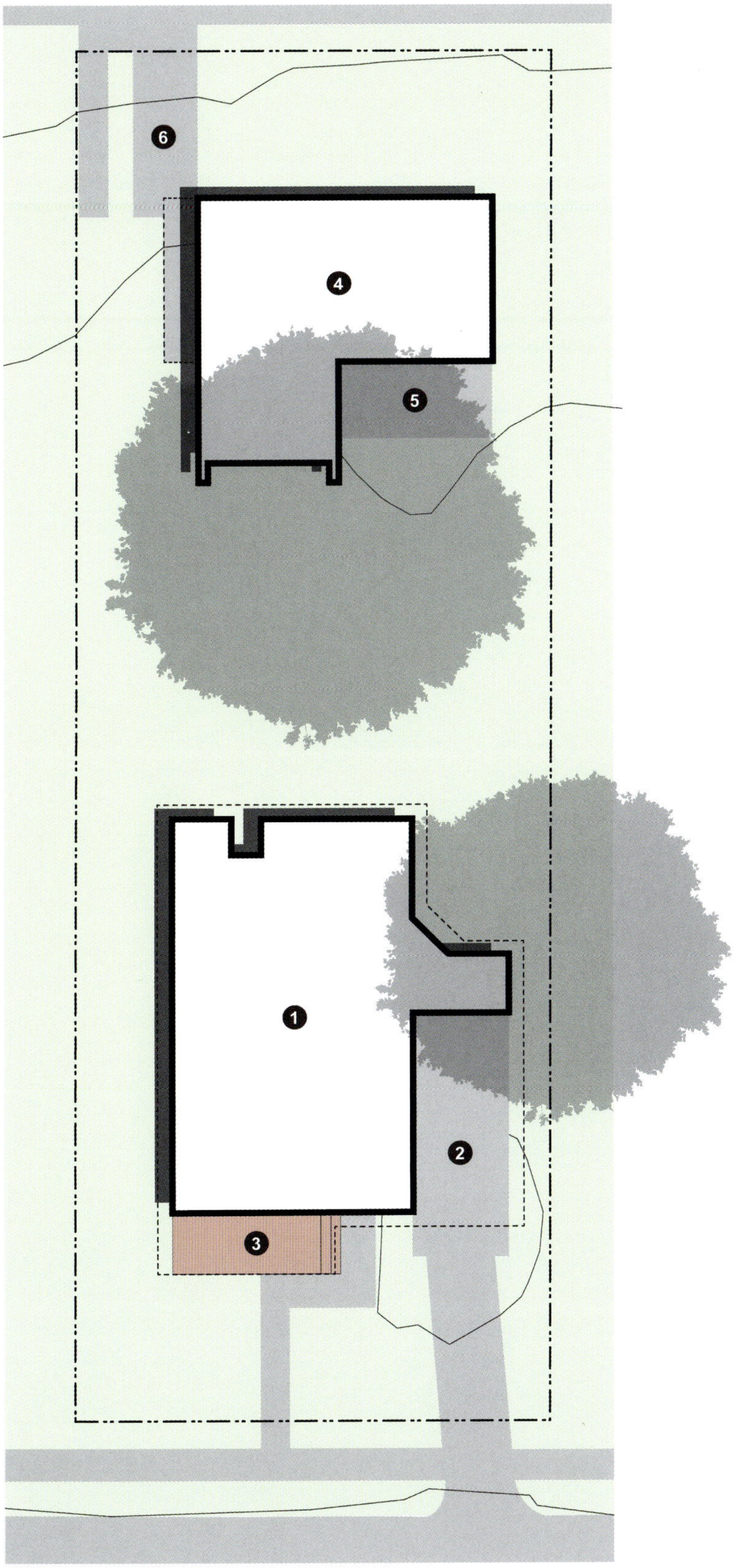

SITE PLAN

1. Main House
2. Main House Drive
3. Main House Porch
4. ADU
5. ADU Porch
6. ADU Drive

PLENTY

A HEALING RETREAT

Created for bodywork classes, a studio in Vancouver, British Columbia, keeps the focus on the physical structure of humans.

PHOTOS COURTESY OF JANIS NICOLAY

Janet, a Feldenkrais instructor, stands in the studio's kitchen, which has two rows of upper cabinets to provide lots of storage.

Janet, a Feldenkrais instructor who lives in East Vancouver, British Columbia, wanted a space bigger than her basement to teach bodywork classes. To provide her architect, Marianne Amodio of MA+HG Architects, a better idea of what the laneway house—the Canadian term for ADU—would be used for, Janet did a hands-on session with her. After Janet demonstrated how she made subtle adjustments to people, Amodio said, "We have to show the bones!"

"It was a very interesting experience," says Amodio. "I immediately started to have ideas about the architecture and expressing the structural design on the interior." She created an exposed roof structure, whose ridge and rafters are roughly analogous to the spine and ribs of the body. Amodio, who chafes against city regulations that limit the designs of laneway houses, also wanted to push the rules in the quest of architectural diversity. She knew that she could maximize the height of the one-story, 615-square-foot studio by giving it a pitched roof, since the city calculated the height of a sloped roof at its midpoint, rather than its apex. But she switched things up by creating a roof with a ridge that runs diagonally between opposing corners, instead of down the center. As a result, while the laneway house does have a pitched roof, it looks nothing like a traditional gabled dwelling.

Inside the building, this unorthodox design draws attention to the exposed structure of Douglas fir timbers and the height of the space, which is 14 feet tall at its highest point. On the outside, the laneway house provides a strong contemporary counterpoint to the main house, a 1930s Craftsman. The cladding is corrugated metal, with a white powder-coated factory finish that the architects placed on a diagonal for visual interest. The same material is used for the roof and the siding, so that it appears to wrap continuously around the building.

Amodio also maximized the amount of floor space for Janet's Feldenkrais classes by carefully banking all the other functions—

An existing vintage apple tree required extra care during construction to avoid damage. A small part of the laneway house's foundation is cantilevered to protect the root zone of the tree.

MA+HG's paper model shows how the roof ridge runs diagonally across the rectangular building. The exterior cladding is also laid diagonally for visual interest.

kitchen, bathroom, bedroom, laundry, and storage—along the walls. When all the doors are closed, these functions disappear and project only 3 feet deep into the main space. As a result, the studio is easy to keep neat and uncluttered, and there is room for eleven people to lie down on the floor for classes and be "mesmerized by the ceiling," says Janet. "You can push the Murphy bed up and everything can go away, and it can stay looking as great as it does in photographs," she adds. "Coming into a space that's expansive and filled with light is healing and invites people to be themselves."

The laneway house also serves as a pavilion where Janet and her husband, Chris, can host parties and large gatherings; in nice weather, fifty people can mingle between the laneway house and its patio. The couple's daughter and her partner have stayed here for a month at a time, and they themselves contemplate moving in after Chris retires. "I have an ongoing appreciation for its pristine quality, spaciousness, and functionality," says Janet.

A tall cabinet next to the front door, which is just out of frame to the left, serves as a hall closet.

A window seat provides a spot to relax and enjoy the garden.

The compact bathroom is split into two rooms; one contains the toilet and sink, and the other has a shower and bench.

A small window over the kitchen sink looks out at the foliage of a strategically placed planter box in the alleyway.

The studio's Murphy bed swings up when not in use. The floor is the polished concrete slab of the home's foundation, which has been embedded with a radiant heating system.

The laneway house can be accessed from an alleyway and has its own parking pad, which doubles as a patio. The front door is set back at an angle to create a small overhang, which is called out with bright-yellow paint.

A glass front door, next to sliding glass doors, ensures that the studio is filled with natural light.

0
5
10
20

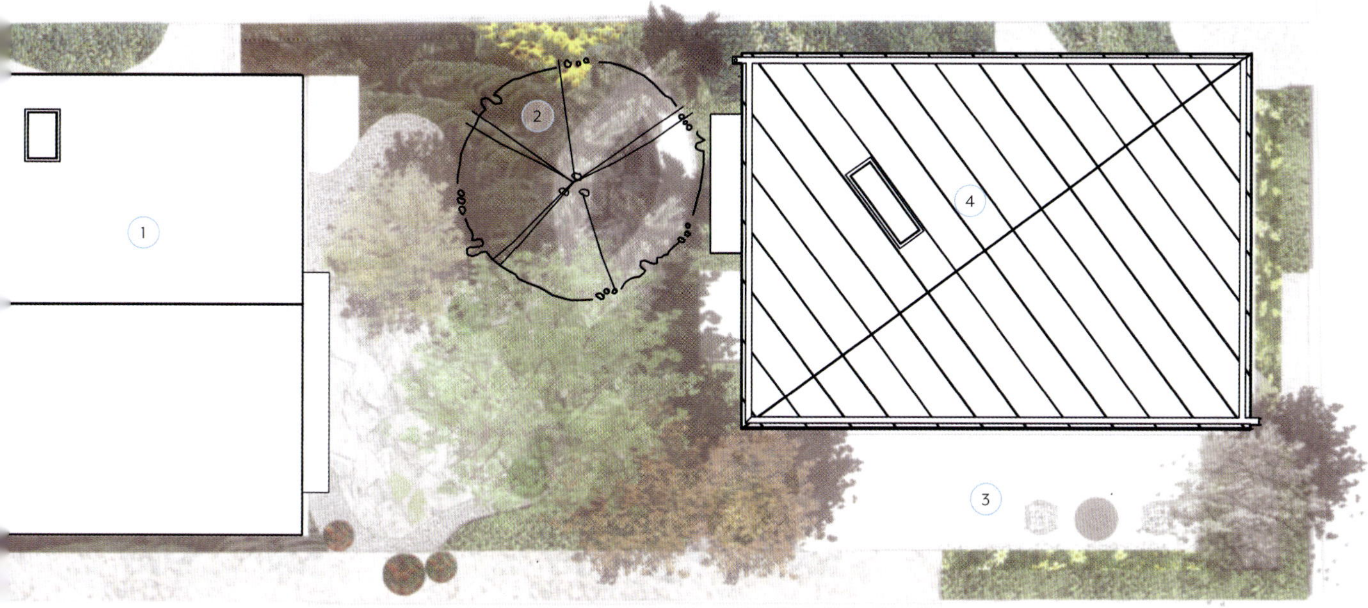

SITE PLAN
1. Principal Dwelling
2. Heritage Apple Tree
3. Patio
4. Laneway Home

GROUND FLOOR
1. Overhang
2. Kitchen
3. Dining/Living Area
4. Murphy Bed
5. Toilet Room
6. Shower Room
7. Window Seat

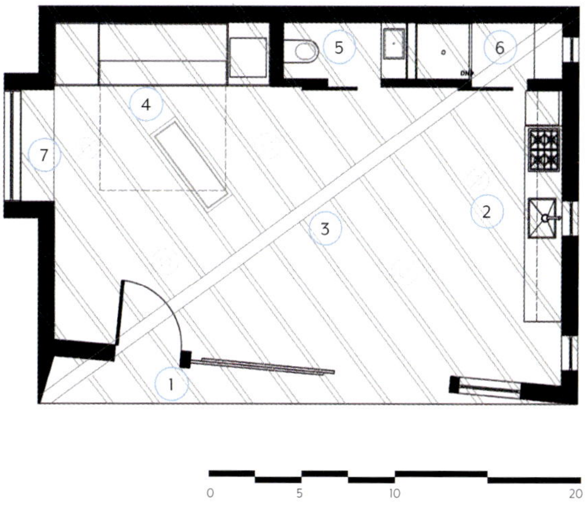

CLOSER TO FAMILY

A city planner creates a long-term housing strategy for himself and his parents in San Jose, California.

PHOTOS COURTESY OF ABODU

For the color of his new ADU, Vu-Bang chose "Cyberspace" gray.

In Asian cultures, children are expected to look after their parents as they age. Vu-Bang, a city planning consultant, is the only child of Vietnamese refugees, and their future was weighing on his mind. He decided to create the modern version of a multigenerational family compound. "The idea was that I would build the unit for me now, but it would potentially be something for my parents later," he says.

For Vu-Bang, building an ADU next to his parents' house in the suburbs of San Jose, California, was a natural extension of their existing relationship. He had been living mostly in L.A. but would come up frequently to the San Francisco Bay Area for work and stay with his parents. Figuring out what his ADU would look like also came easily. While he was consulting for the cities of Napa and Sonoma and helping them develop ADU guidelines, he had come across a photo of an ADU that he admired. "I really wish I could build this," he recalls thinking. "But I thought it was going to be by a crazy Scandinavian company who built them in fjords."

The compact home has pitched ceilings that go up to more than 10 feet, making the space feel larger.

When the ADU arrived on-site, the kitchen was already installed, including all the appliances.

Vu-Bang was not actually that far off. The ADU had been designed by an English firm called Koto. But it was a prefab ADU offered by Abodu, a company conveniently located in the Bay Area. They had three models—a studio, a one-bedroom, and a two-bedroom—which were preapproved by the city of San Jose. And his parents' home had a big backyard that overlooked rolling hills. By placing the ADU perpendicular to one end of the two-story house, both the ADU and main house could have good views. "The site worked really well for two structures," says Kent Baltare, Abodu's vice president of operations.

Vu-Bang chose Abodu's one-bedroom, one-bath ADU. To pay for it, his parents took out a home equity loan and Vu-Bang made the monthly loan payments. Like the company's other models, the 500-square-foot dwelling is completely powered by electricity and is built to maximize energy efficiency; the units exceed the requirements of California's Title 24 energy code, which are the most stringent in the country. "It's definitely much higher quality construction than if I had it built," says Vu-Bang. "I don't think I would be able to afford this level of architecture." He wanted the ADU to support aging in place, so he upgraded the unit to a zero-threshold shower; Abodu's ADUs come standard with enlarged doorways that accommodate wheelchairs.

Vu-Bang was also pleased with how quickly the ADU came together, even in the midst of a pandemic. He signed the contract in December 2019, the ADU arrived on-site in June 2020, and he moved in a month later. Since then, he has given up his place in L.A. and moved in full-time; his fiancée will be joining him soon. "It's definitely reduced the level of anxiety about the long-term plan," he says. "We have at least the next decade planned out."

The bathroom has a pocket door to save space.

PREFAB OR STICK-BUILT?

Because they are constructed in a factory, prefab ADUs—also called "modular ADUs"—can offer better quality and lower pricing than custom ADUs. According to Abodu's Baltare, prefab saves at least 20 percent compared to custom. But he says the main benefit is really the time saved. A custom project takes seven to twelve months of on-site construction, compared to one month for prefab. "We offer a much-faster timeline to getting a super-high-quality ADU," says Baltare. "Customers are sensitive to how their neighbors will react to a second home in their backyard, and don't want to become the villain of the neighborhood because of construction noise."

Abodu also offers customers a single point of contact for these complex projects. The company handles the permitting, site work (includes excavating a shallow crawlspace and laying a perimeter foundation), installation, connecting the utilities, and final inspection. "People are not looking to be construction project managers," says Baltare.

Prefab homes definitely have their drawbacks. Since they are predesigned, their floor plans are set, and customization is very limited. Choices of fixtures and finishes—including lights, faucets, flooring, and tile—are also typically restricted to a few options. And because the ADU will be delivered on a truck bed and craned into place, your property needs to have enough access, which a prefab company will determine beforehand.

An angled ceiling in the bedroom creates architectural interest in the modest structure.

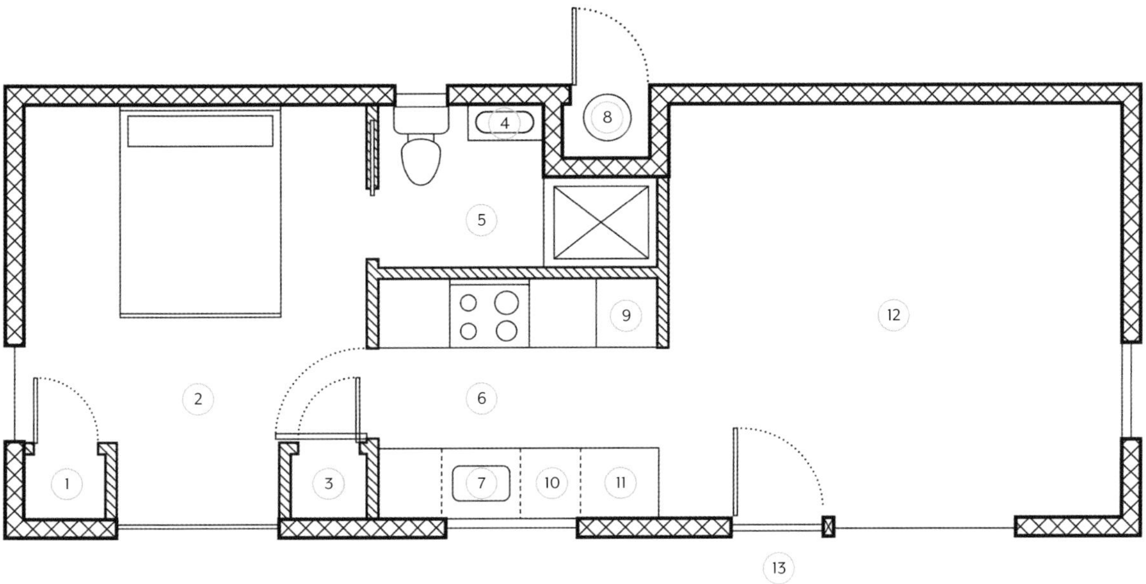

1. Closet
2. Bedroom
3. Closet
4. Sink
5. Bathroom
6. Kitchen
7. Sink
8. Water Heater
9. Fridge
10. Dishwasher
11. Washer/Dryer
12. Living/Dining Room
13. Main Entrance

The ADU has operable casement windows for natural ventilation.

ARTISTIC FREEDOM

A new house in Los Angeles has a separate studio for creative chaos.

PHOTOS COURTESY OF ERIC STAUDENMAIER

A set of large metal doors allow the ADU to function as a one-car garage if necessary.

Nearly every single day, someone walking by Mo and Gavin's house in L.A.'s Mar Vista neighborhood will stop to take a picture of their house. More specifically, passersby are training their cameras at their ADU, which is painted fire-engine red and has a pointy roof.

Both the ADU and the main house were designed by local architecture and design studio ORA, providing a place for calm and orderly living as well as a dedicated space to make a mess. Mo is a TV and film production executive who spends a lot of time with spreadsheets, while Gavin is an artist; the two of them have a young daughter who also enjoys painting. "I'm a neat freak, and then I have two artists who live with me. The art studio is their space to go wild," explains Mo.

Originally, the couple planned to build a prefab home because they wanted to minimize construction waste and keep costs down. The prefab model had a built-in garage that they were going to use as an art studio. However, quite late into the process, the prefab company told them that the model they had picked wouldn't fit on their site. So Mo and Gavin turned to architects Oonagh Ryan and James Guillou of ORA to see if they could build something custom that was still close to the original budget. In the end, the cost of custom was about 25 percent more than the prefab price but included a separate ADU / art studio in addition to all the custom-designed features. "They wanted a lot, and we were able to get them there in a way that's smart yet simple and, I think, attainable," says Ryan. "Most of our clients have ambitious ideas and tight budgets, so we design in parallel as we are developing budgets and make sure to have the contractor on board in the early phases of design."

The ADU's north-facing trapezoidal skylight illuminates the art studio. The concrete floor is the polished slab of the foundation.

After you enter the foyer, a door to the right leads to the ADU, while the main house is to the left.

Gavin, an artist, was sensitive to the quality of light in the studio. Inspired by artist James Turrell's Skyspaces, the architects created a trapezoidal skylight that brings in bright but diffused light. The 17-foot-high ceiling accommodates larger artworks. The ADU's red hue was taken directly from a strawberry plant that Mo and Gavin grew at the cottage they previously lived in. The architects found an elastomeric roof coating that could be painted red and matched the texture of the ADU's stucco walls. "Every single inch of this project is uniquely 'them,'" says Guillou.

Because the ORA team designed the 2,100-square-foot house and 300-square-foot ADU at the same time, they were able to organize them strategically to create outdoor living areas. The studio doubles as a pool house and hangout for kids, opening to the back patio and a lap pool through sliding glass doors. While the ADU has large doors on the front, the family usually accesses it from a door in the foyer of the main house. "I would never now think of a home without having a space like that," says Mo. "It's their happy space."

PARKING IN DISGUISE

While most cities require homes to have a driveway or garage for parking cars off the street, urban planners are rethinking our car-centric approach when it comes to ADUs. Depending on where you live, you may not have to use up valuable real estate on parking. In California, for instance, if the ADU is within a half mile of public transit or meets other conditions, you don't need to provide a dedicated parking spot for the ADU.

Because of their proximity to public transportation, Gavin and Mo didn't need to provide a parking spot for their ADU. But they did need to provide two covered parking spots for their new house, which ORA fulfilled by technically creating a one-car garage with a carport in front. The ADU has a pair of doors in front that can swing open, and the trellis currently shades a sitting area that can become a parking spot if needed.

The strawberry-red building has attracted the attention of many passersby.

The ADU and house, which were designed together, are arranged around a pool. A retractable awning system can be extended to provide shade over the pool patio.

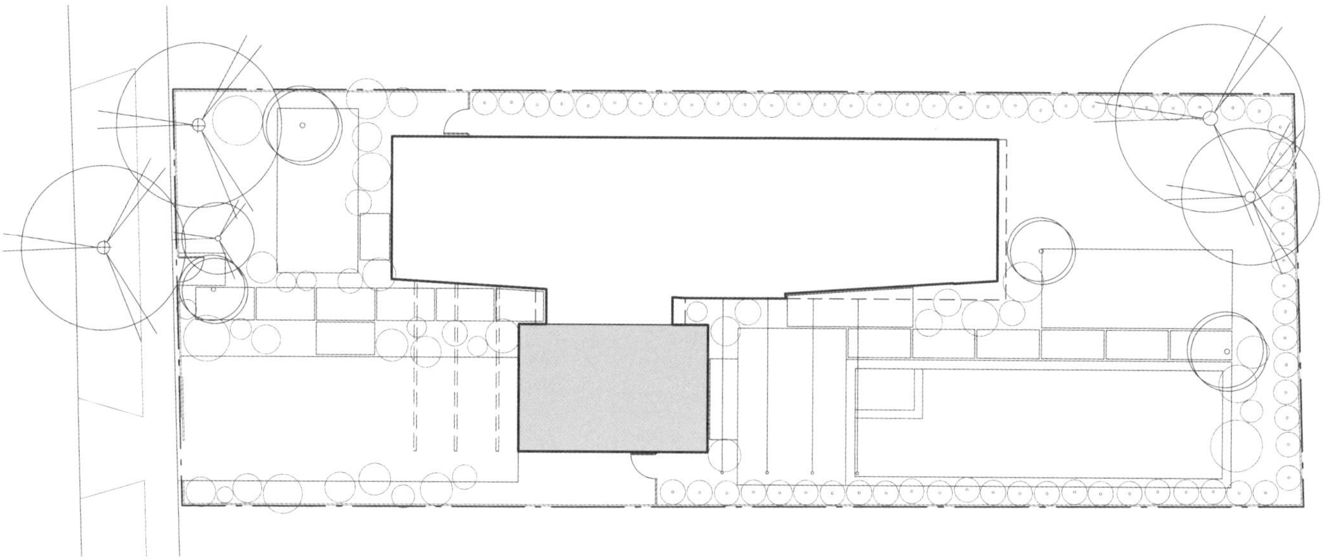

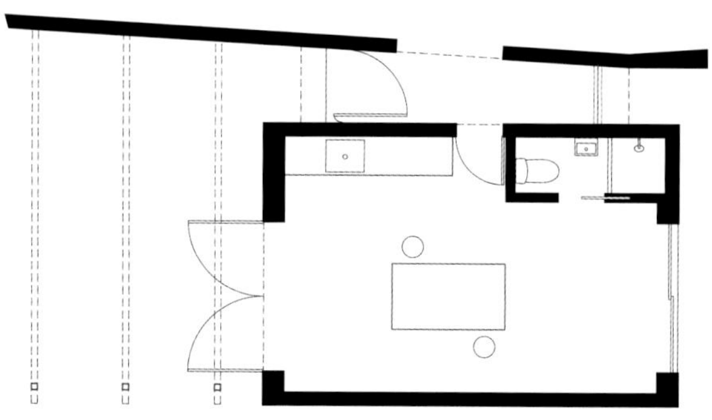

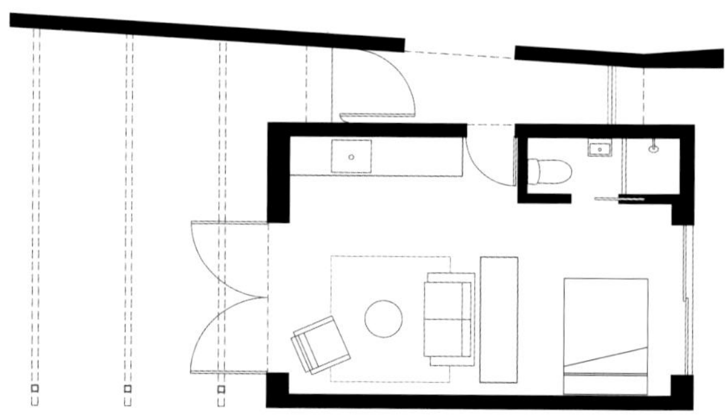

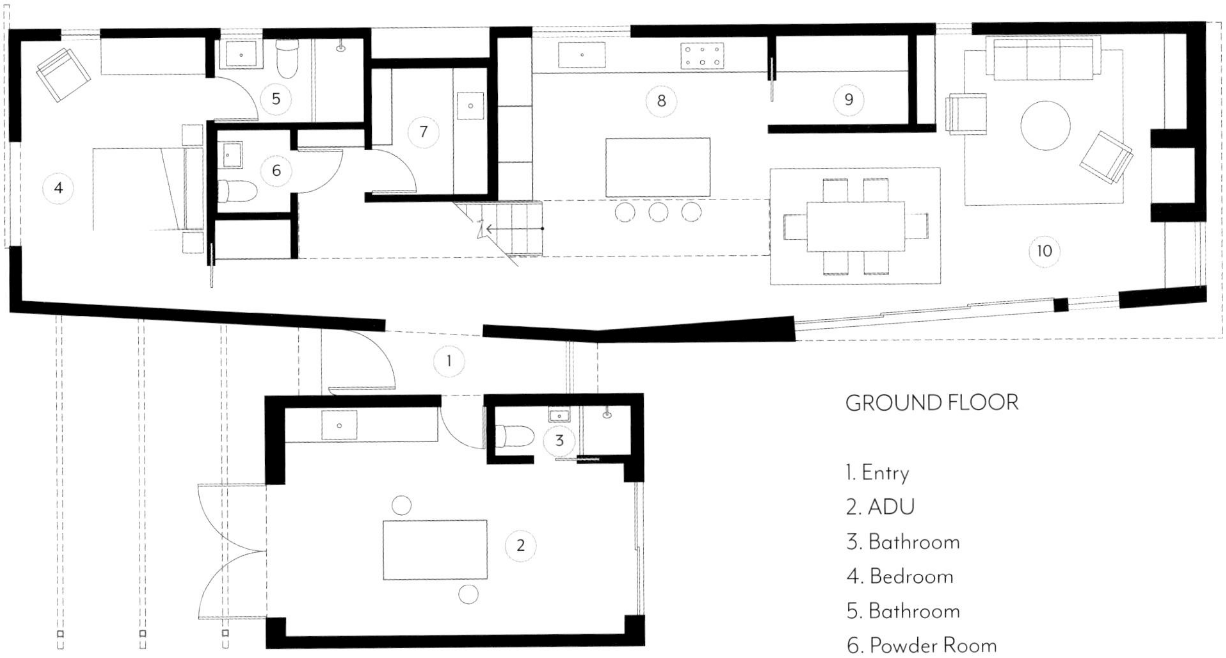

GROUND FLOOR

1. Entry
2. ADU
3. Bathroom
4. Bedroom
5. Bathroom
6. Powder Room
7. Laundry
8. Kitchen
9. Pantry
10. Living/Dining

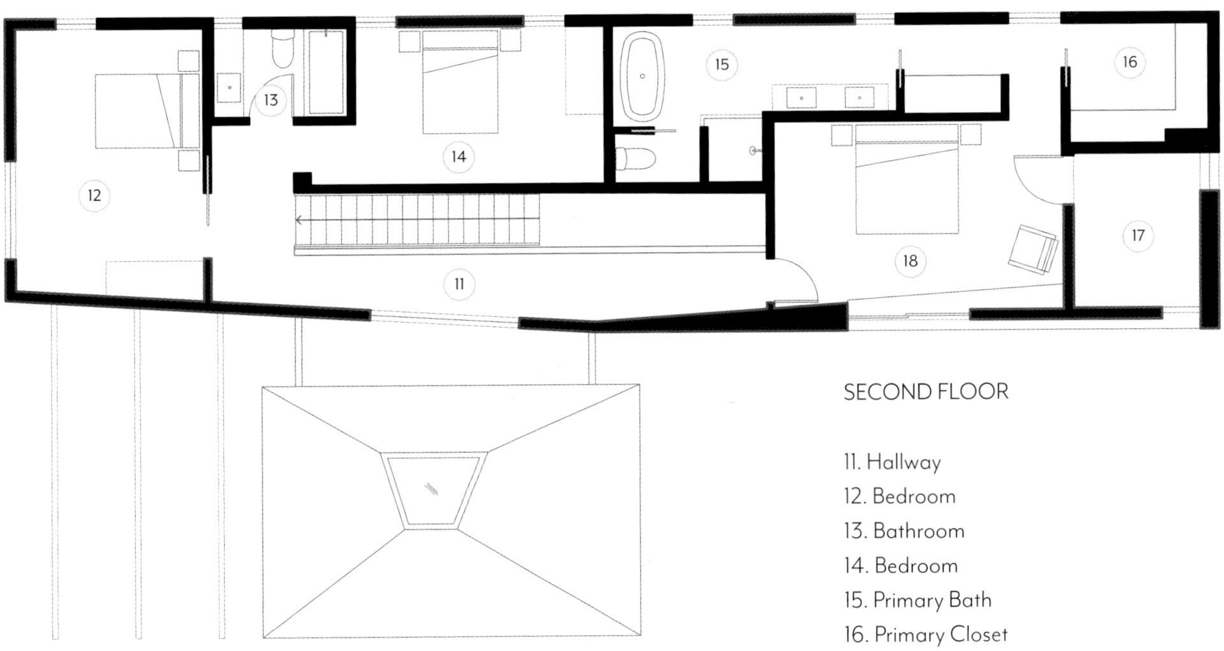

SECOND FLOOR

11. Hallway
12. Bedroom
13. Bathroom
14. Bedroom
15. Primary Bath
16. Primary Closet
17. Deck
18. Primary Bedroom

HERE COMES THE SUN

A Seattle ADU keeps the gloom away.

PHOTOS COURTESY OF MARK WOODS PHOTOGRAPHY

Because of the roof's asymmetric shape, each main space inside has a distinct character. Plywood lining the lower level provides a sense of intimacy within the double-height ADU.

The sheltered front porch, lined with cedar, faces the alleyway. Inside, the space above the porch is used to store the couple's camping gear.

Leesa and Ben, a couple in their fifties, loved their 1906 Craftsman in the Ballard neighborhood of Seattle. But the small vintage home was dark and cramped. It also had no upstairs bathroom and a really steep staircase, resulting in perilous journeys in the middle of the night. "We joke that the house must have been built by a drunken sailor," says Leesa.

After learning how much it would cost to fix these nontrivial problems, the couple decided to invest in an ADU first. They figured they could rent it out, and if they decided to proceed with the home renovation, they would have somewhere to live during the construction. The couple also contemplated moving into the ADU after they retired, when they looked forward to spending a good portion of the year in the Southwest and sunnier climes.

The couple approached SHED Architecture & Design to create an architecturally interesting ADU. To help them age in place, they requested that all the main spaces be located on the ground floor. The architects obliged with an 800-square-foot, one-bedroom structure that has a soaring, asymmetrical roof that creates different

A large sliding glass door connects the ADU with the garden outside.

volumes over each of the main spaces. The high ceiling, which goes up more than 17 feet, provides room for a small loft where the couple enjoys listening to their collection of vinyl records; it is also an additional sleeping area. The corner next to the front door is carved in to create a sheltered porch; it was also a strategic way to reduce the amount of square footage so that the ADU stayed within the maximum allowed by the city.

For their sun-loving clients, the design team brightened the dwelling with a row of four roof windows, which can easily be opened by going into the loft and reaching up. An additional skylight illuminates the bathroom, which is on the ground level and looks up at the 17-foot-tall ceiling. Instead of a roof deck, which the clients didn't think they would use, the architects created a gently sloping, south-facing section of the roof that is optimized for future solar panels.

As designed, the ADU threatened to exceed the couple's budget. The architects sketched out some simple alternatives that would

The side of the ADU that faces the main house is mostly opaque, creating privacy between the two buildings.

have been less costly to build, but Ben and Leesa had fallen in love with the vision. To keep costs down, a friend of the couple who was a general contractor got the project started and coached Leesa so that she could take over the job. Leesa, who is a mycologist, had the patience from reading scientific papers to learn about construction details. "It was great having a really energized client who was able to make it happen and had fun building the thing that they wanted," says architect Prentis Hale of SHED. "They put in the sweat equity and a lot of love into it, so the ADU is truly theirs."

Although their original plan was to continue living in the Craftsman, the couple moved into the ADU almost immediately. "After two days, we knew that renting it out was not going to happen," says Leesa. Because of the amount of sun that comes into the ADU, overcast days during the winter no longer feel as oppressive to the couple. Says Leesa, "It just shows you when you use space wisely, you can live so much larger."

The kitchen is outfitted with IKEA cabinetry that has been customized with plywood fronts. The polished concrete floor is heated with a hydronic heating system.

Natural ventilation and fans do a good job of keeping the house cool. The ADU also has a heat pump that provides air-conditioning when necessary. The casement window provides a cleaner, uninterrupted view compared to a traditional window with a sliding sash.

The bathroom is designed as a wet room, so the shower doesn't require a dividing wall from the tub or toilet. Leesa and Ben, self-described "bath people," wanted a deep soaking tub that could fit them both.

SKYLIGHT OPTIONS

Skylights are useful for bringing in more natural light, particularly in situations where there isn't that much natural light to begin with. Skylights can be fixed, which means that they don't open, or operable, which means that they do. Some manufacturers offer motorized skylights that can be opened by remote control. Roof windows, which are sometimes called "venting skylights," are manually operable skylights that can be easily opened for natural ventilation.

The roof windows in Leesa and Ben's ADU pivot 180 degrees around a center axis, instead of hinging from one end. The center pivot allows the roof windows to be easily pushed open, and they can be opened wide enough to stick your head out or even access the roof. Because they pivot, they are also easier to clean. To cool down the space in the summer, Leesa opens a roof window and a window on the lower level, so that hot air flows out of the space via the chimney effect.

A rendering of the ADU shows where the solar panels will be installed.

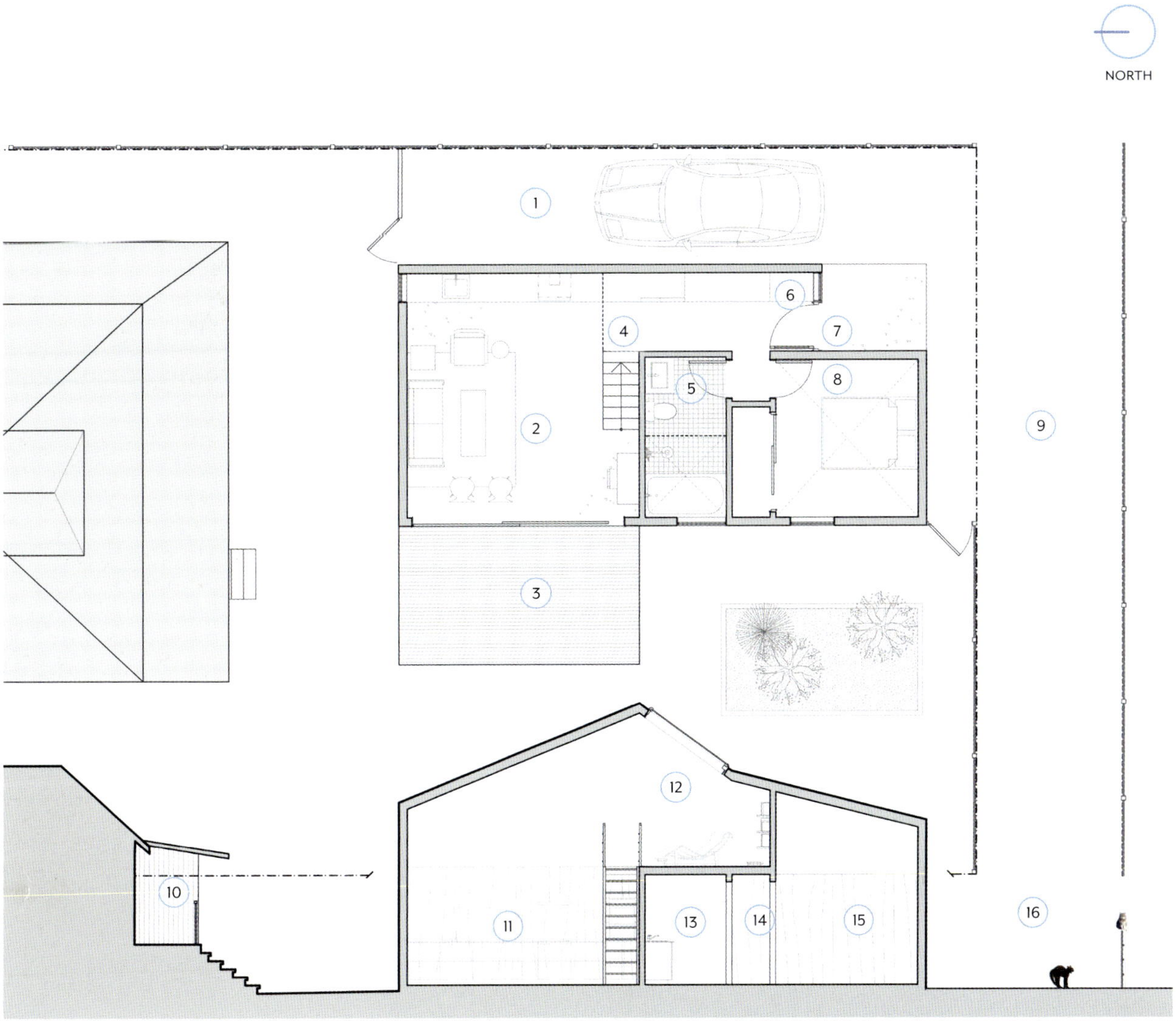

1. Driveway
2. Living Room / Kitchen
3. Patio
4. Loft Above
5. Bath
6. Bench
7. Entry
8. Bedroom
9. Alley

10. Primary House
11. Living Room / Kitchen
12. Loft
13. Bath
14. Hall
15. Bedroom
16. Alley

PEAK PERFORMANCE

An ADU in California's Marin County navigates a small, steep site.

PHOTOS COURTESY OF BRUCE DAMONTE

Fiber-cement panels in a light gray, which are used for the roof as well as the siding, have begun to patina like concrete. "It's an ingenious option that gives you the concrete look but is also very practical," says Andrew.

Located on a steep hillside in San Anselmo, Andrew and Elena's house is hard to get to, let alone build upon. But the remote feeling of the forested setting is what inspired the couple, who are based in San Francisco, to purchase the property as a weekend retreat—even though it needed a lot of work. The dated 1950s main house was billed an "investment opportunity" and was accompanied by an unfinished ADU.

Elena and Andrew, both of whom work in the tech industry, decided to contact the ADU's architect to help complete it. As it turns out, the architect was Casper Mork-Ulnes, who has a long history designing small dwellings. In 2004, he founded a company called Modern Cabana, specializing in prefab backyard structures, which he later sold. "Fitting a lot of stuff into a small footprint is an interesting problem for us," he says. The original client asked Mork-Ulnes and his team to create an ADU on the 312-square-foot foundation of the house's garage, and that it include a separate bedroom for his daughter. The architects also had to contend with the steep hillside behind the garage, which limited the site's exposure to natural light.

The design handles both constraints, carving out both light and space. The ADU is essentially a studio apartment, and necessities for living are carefully organized along two walls, including a Murphy bed. But it also has a small loft area that can function as an additional bedroom. The roof soars upward to peek over the crest of the hill, bringing light in through operable clerestory windows. The architects also added a deck that extends the ADU's limited space outside.

A row of clerestory windows wash the ceiling with light and balance out the light coming through the sliding glass doors. Marine-grade Douglas fir plywood was bleached with lye—a traditional Scandinavian technique for lightening wood—so that it complements the gray exterior. The concrete floor is a skim coat over the garage foundation.

Because it has locking casters, the kitchen island can easily change locations and transform into a dining table.

A meticulously designed wall of built-ins also conceals the ADU's electrical heating and cooling system. "The Mork-Ulnes style is that they don't like to have any trim—achieving zero reveals and 1/16-inch clearances requires a lot of attention to detail on the part of the builder," says Andrew.

Because Andrew and Elena got involved before the ADU was completed, they were able to make some modifications to the original design. They opted for a dishwasher instead of a stacked washer and dryer and installed an under-the-counter fridge in lieu of a full-size fridge in favor of more counter space. To give them even more counter space, the architects designed a kitchen island on wheels. When it's parallel to the rest of the kitchen, it's an island, and when it's perpendicular, it's a dining table. Instead of a front door and tiny foyer, there is now a built-in sofa and storage cubbies, and the entrance is through the sliding glass doors.

The couple plans to renovate the main house with the help of Mork-Ulnes Architects and spend most of their weekends in the ADU with their two young children, who share the loft bedroom. "I always wanted to get a camper van, and this house is like one," says Andrew. "It's very compact, and everyone can spend the night packed together in the middle of nature. It's very fun."

A green-tiled shower also opens to the outside, creating the feel of an outdoor shower.

To add functionality to the space, Elena and Andrew added a built-in sofa with storage above and below.

Accessed by a custom ladder, the second-floor office/bedroom is technically a storage space.

Located in the hills of San Anselmo, the ADU is built on the foundation of the main house's garage. The architects added a cantilevered deck, which required some additional foundation work.

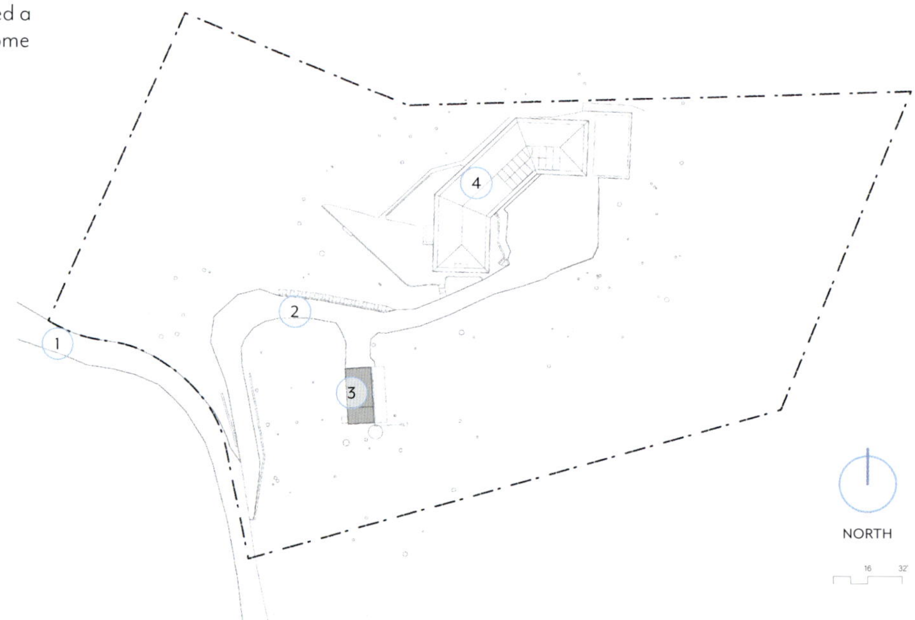

SITE PLAN

1. Road
2. Driveway
3. ADU
4. Main House

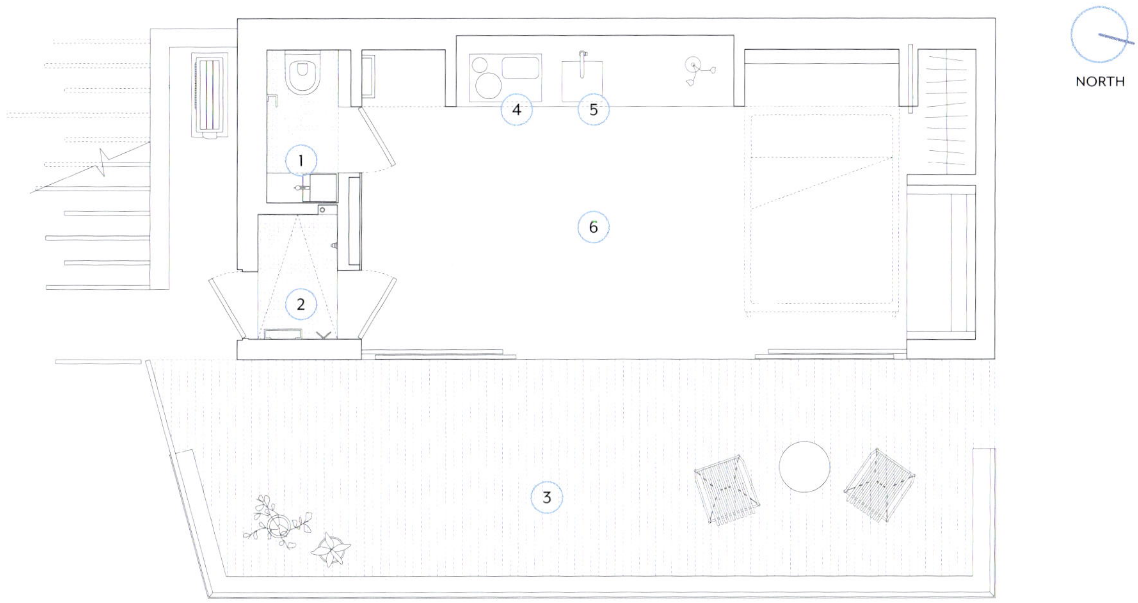

GROUND FLOOR

1. WC
2. Shower
3. Deck
4. Range
5. Sink
6. Living Room / Kitchen / Bedroom

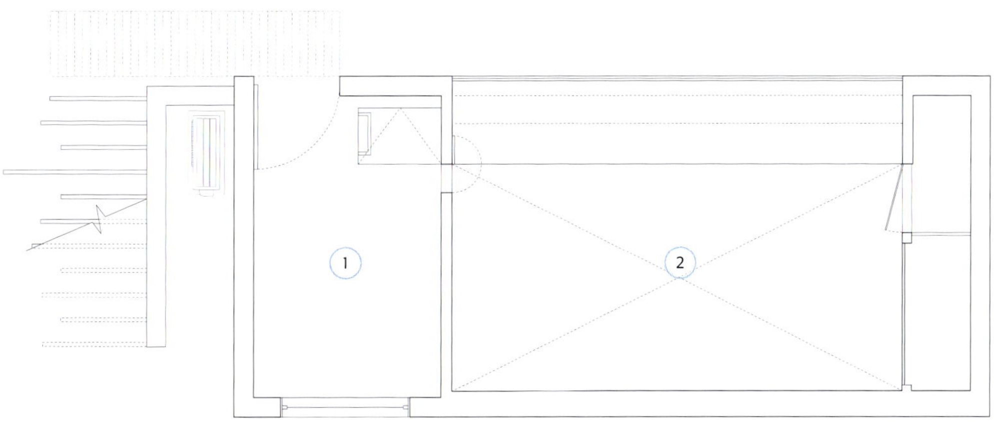

SECOND FLOOR

1. Storage Loft
2. Living Room / Kitchen / Bedroom

PEEKING THROUGH

A garden wall creates privacy and defines outdoor space for an ADU in Austin, Texas.

PHOTOS COURTESY OF CHLOE GILSTRAP OF LIKENESS STUDIO AND LEONID FURMANSKY

Holly chose rift-sawn white oak for the custom cabinetry in the kitchen and storage next to the stairwell, and engineered white oak for the knee space in the kitchen island. The flooring on the upper level is also engineered white oak. *Photo courtesy of Leonid Furmansky*

Before Holly and her husband, Matt, purchased the 1935 Craftsman house in Austin, Texas, it had been occupied by the same owner for seventy years. The vintage, three-bedroom home on the city's East Side suffered from deferred maintenance and needed new wiring and plumbing. The young couple decided that they would build an ADU in the back first, where they could live while tackling the remodel of the front house and invite friends and family in afterward. "We definitely orient our lives around our friends and our community and wanted to make it a place where we could host people," says Holly.

The couple hired architects Arthur Furman and Annie-Laurie Grabiel of Side Angle Side, drawn to the streamlined version of a traditional gabled house that the firm had done previously. The architects' approach is to pare things back: "It's so easy to be additive in architecture, so we just keep simplifying everything up until the point we break ground," says Grabiel. Holly, an interior designer, handled the selection of finishes and furnishings.

The design team pored over the details of a two-level, 1,100-square-foot ADU with a bedroom and bath on each floor.

The cedar siding will eventually weather to a silvery gray. The outdoor light is a custom fixture designed by Holly, an interior designer. *Photo courtesy of Leonid Furmansky*

The simple gable form of the ADU appears over the edge of the garden wall, which is covered in three-part burnished stucco for a smooth finish. The archway on the left leads to the front door. *Photo courtesy of Chloe Gilstrap of Likeness Studio*

The garden wall conceals a covered carport and outdoor dining area. *Photo courtesy of Chloe Gilstrap of Likeness Studio*

Taking every opportunity to add storage, the architects enclosed the stairwell with a storage unit. And while they didn't specifically design the upstairs bedroom closets to fit a portable crib, the closets are big enough to double as nap rooms. These enclosed spaces have since come in handy since the couple has a toddler and another baby on the way.

The architects also looked for ways to add outdoor space. "Any ADU is going to be limited in space," says Furman. "Our strategy was to figure out where the interior could spill out and create the effect of expanding the exterior, almost doubling the space. This ADU has all the program of a main house, even if some of it has to happen outside." The architects placed covered outdoor areas on the eastern side so the house could offer protection from the hot

afternoon sun. They designed a tall garden wall, nearly 40 feet long, which screens off the carport and outdoor dining area of the ADU. The massive concrete divider, which has two openings to also provide a sense of connection between the front and back houses, brings architectural heft to the backyard. "It makes a statement—it's a big, beautiful monolithic wall," says Holly.

As part of their aesthetic, the architects brought in materials that would develop a patina, such as knotty cedar siding. "A lot of new construction is missing the soul," says Furman. "We especially love materials that will degrade over time, like troweled stucco and sunbaked brick," says Grabiel. "Those are some of the things that we used in the ADU to make it feel like it wasn't born yesterday."

Open-sided shelving allows light into the stairwell. *Photo courtesy of Leonid Furmansky*

Holly and Matt sit on the spacious balcony outside their upstairs bedroom. The bedroom is designed as a loft, with a staircase that opens straight into the room, rather than use valuable square footage on a landing to provide a door. *Photo courtesy of Leonid Furmansky*

Instead of tile, the shower is coated in waterproof plaster, which is used to coat pools. The shower bench and vanity countertop are made from a engineered material that resembles concrete. *Photo courtesy of Leonid Furmansky*

The architects designed medicine cabinets that integrate the bathroom window and a vanity paneled in rift-sawn white oak. The backsplash is tiled with tiny unglazed porcelain Japanese tiles that resemble stone. *Photo courtesy of Leonid Furmansky*

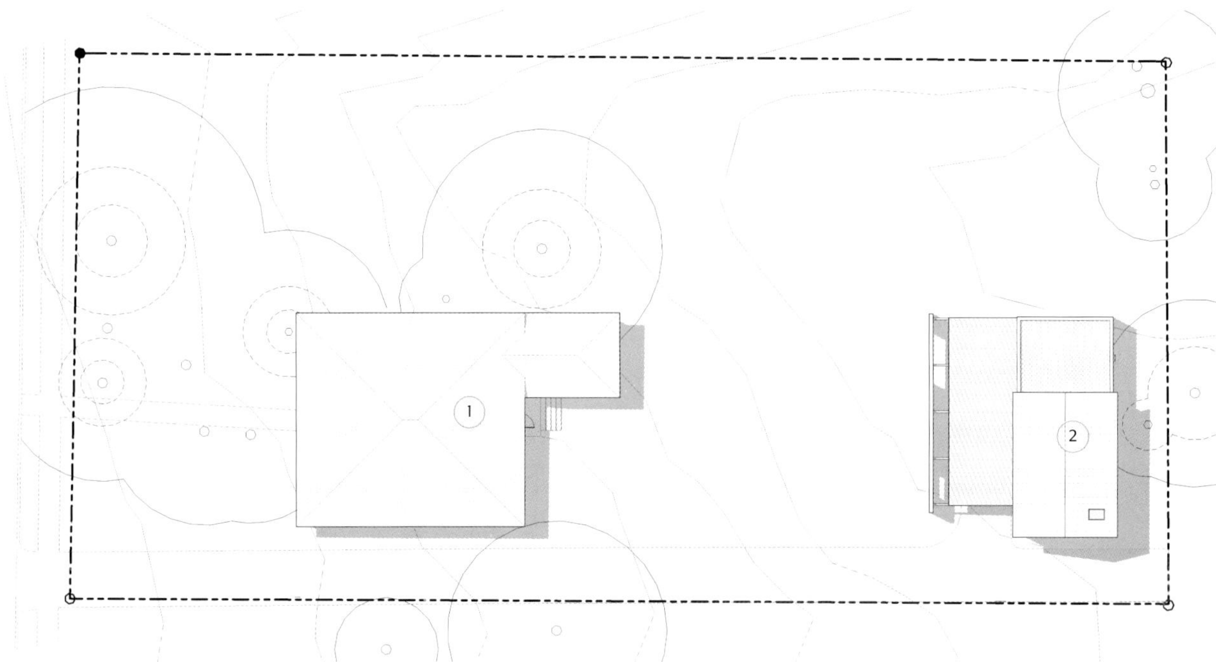

1. Existing Residence
2. ADU

1. Carport
2. Outdoor Dining
3. Living Room
4. Kitchen
5. Bathroom
6. Guest Room
7. Primary Bed
8. Closet
9. Primary Bath
10. Balcony

BREAKING OUT OF THE BOX

An author creates his ideal writing studio in the San Francisco Bay Area.

PHOTOS COURTESY OF BRUCE DAMONTE

The ADU's glass-walled living room opens onto a small private deck.

The mat foundation has a cantilevered edge, giving the small structure a dynamic quality.

Before he published his first novel, Mike had an established career as an art director, creating advertisements for everything from cars to ice cream. Given his design background, he had high expectations for the writing studio he wanted to build in his Bay Area backyard. "I wanted it to be something that was inspiring and forward-thinking, not something that I could conceive of myself," he says.

IwamotoScott Architecture was up for the challenge, creating a 640-square-foot studio ADU that is both practical and interesting to look at. The split-level structure has a many-faceted shape: In addition to its six sides, it has an unusual roofline that dips up and down like a large check mark. The form is a response to the irregular, sloping site, allowing the ADU to fit within local height limitations and capture the best views. "There are no real right angles in the plan—the shape is improvisational," says architect Craig Scott. The small building also forwards the architectural dialogue started by the main house, a midcentury Eichler home with a low gabled roof and plenty of glass walls.

Most of the ADU is clad in lightly charred cedar.

From inside, the functionality of the design is readily apparent. Mike's built-in desk. located on a raised platform, is positioned just so to see Mount Diablo in the distance. To contain the hundreds of books in Mike's collection, the architects designed walls of built-ins and a large freestanding bookcase that also contains a gas fireplace and a TV. Push-open doors clad in walnut veneer keep everything hidden out of sight. An alcove behind his desk, lit by a skylight, holds a small garden.

"When I come here, I'm in a different frame of mind," says Mike, who is currently finishing his second novel while continuing his consulting business. "My work can be chaotic and very fast paced, and this orderly space tamps all that down and provides a respite. The amazing thing about architecture is that it can transport you somewhere else."

The walnut built-ins conceal a television and Mike's large library. The fireplace supplements the ADU's in-floor radiant heating,

Behind the built-in desk is a small garden.

ANDRE FU
CAPITOL RECORDS

From his desk, Mike can look through the kitchen window and through a gap in the roofline of the main house for a view across the San Francisco Bay.

The bath features a walnut vanity and a shower lined with a large-format porcelain tile that resembles onyx.

From the bathroom door, you look down a hallway to the indoor landscape.

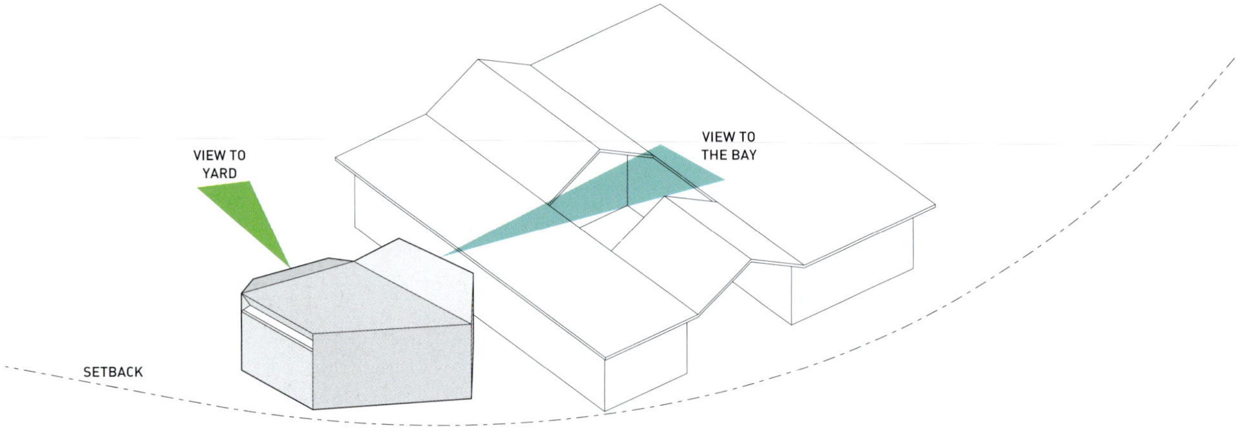

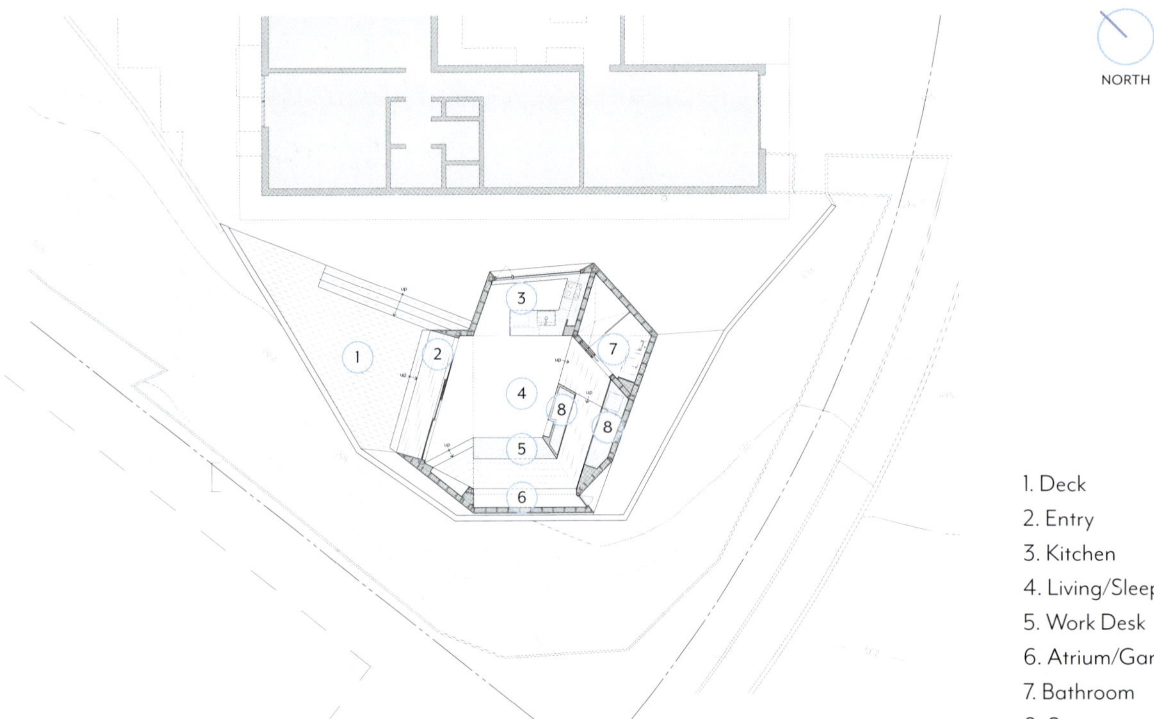

1. Deck
2. Entry
3. Kitchen
4. Living/Sleeping
5. Work Desk
6. Atrium/Garden
7. Bathroom
8. Storage

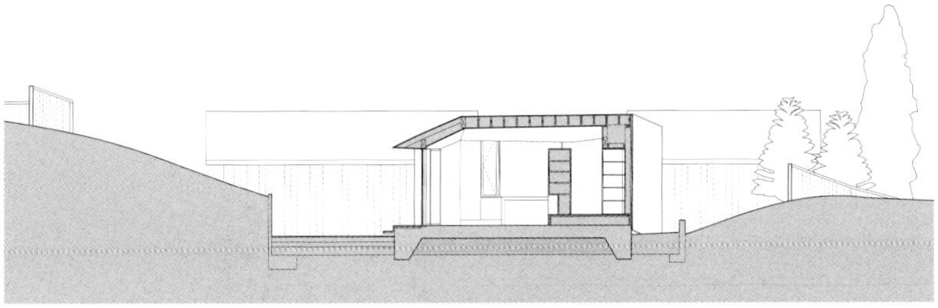

Building Section, SW–NE

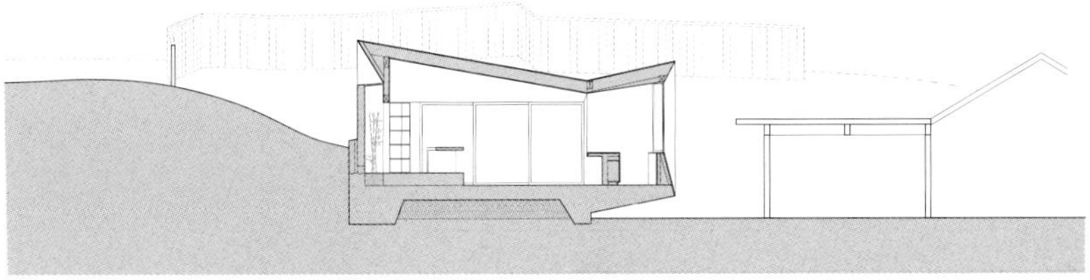

Building Section, NW–SE,

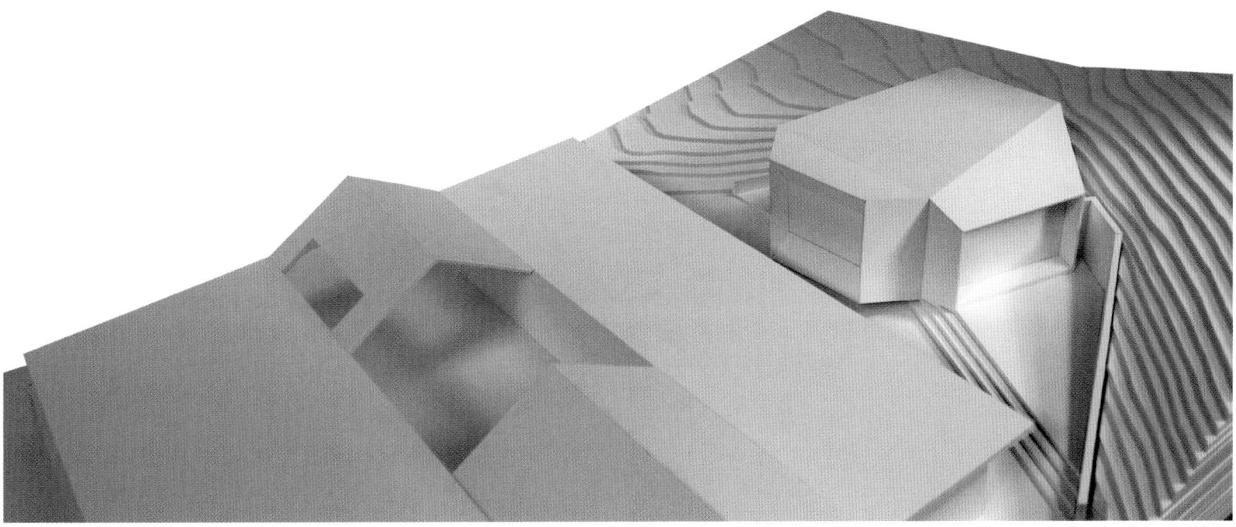

GREEN INSIDE AND OUT

An architect couple investigates the latest construction techniques in Ann Arbor, Michigan.

PHOTOS COURTESY OF CHRIS MIELE

To bring sun in and keep the space cool during midwestern summers, the ADU has three operable skylights: two in the living area and one in the bathroom.

A few years back, Adam Fure and Ellie Abrons, who teach architecture at the University of Michigan in Ann Arbor, decided to test-drive the city's new ADU regulations by building one as a rental property at their own home. They had just started a small architecture firm called T+E+A+M with two colleagues, and the ADU was also an opportunity to test some new construction materials and systems.

Fure and Abrons live on the west side of town in the Eberwhite neighborhood, in a 1952 house that they share with their two kids. At the time, the city required ADUs to be part of the main house or other existing structure. Consequently, the architects designed a 730-square-foot ADU that extends back from the home's garage. To preserve most of their backyard, the architects created a two-story ADU with a loft bedroom rather than put all the spaces on one level. Their goal was to construct an extremely energy-efficient dwelling as affordably as possible.

To reduce the costs of one major component of home construction, T+E+A+M used an innovative foundation developed in Scandinavia, which Fure describes as a "simple and smart system." Because ground shifts when it freezes and thaws, foundations in cold climates like Michigan's are typically excavated below the frost line. An alternative to digging a crawlspace or basement and then hiring a mason to build the space is to use a frost-protected shallow foundation starting with a layer of gravel that is topped by a thick layer of foam insulation, and a concrete slab foundation poured on top of that.

The architects were also curious to see if building the ADU from prefabricated structural insulated panels (SIPs) was a better approach than traditional framing. The savings with SIPs comes from reducing construction time, and the ADU came together quickly, taking a crew of five people only three days to build the structure.

The exposed ceiling showcases the engineered wood, including ceiling joists of laminated strand lumber (LSL) that was used to build the ADU.

The ADU at architects Adam Fure and Ellie Abrons's home has an industrial simplicity. On the lower level, steel mesh panels will someday be covered with vines, creating a green wall.

"You can get a tenant in that much more quickly and start bringing in rental income, which is the economic proposition for panelized systems in ADUs," says Fure. The SIPs with the frost-protected shallow foundation were a winning combination. "The continuous insulation of the foundation system and the SIPs produces a really airtight, energy-efficient shell," says Fure, who notes that the ADU uses very little energy for heating and cooling.

The exterior of the ADU is designed for durability and aesthetic appeal on a budget. They clad the upper level with fiber-cement panels, while on the lower level they coated the SIPs with liquid vapor barrier, painted them with UV-resistant paint, and installed steel mesh panels. Since then, they've planted vines that have grown over the mesh and covered the facade for what Fure describes as "the DIY version of a living wall."

The stair treads were cut from 3.5-inch-thick laminated strand lumber. Originally, the architects planned to expose the oriented strand board (OSB) of the SIPs, but when the surfaces of the panels were a little too grungy even for their tastes, they added a thin OSB veneer to interior surfaces.

Rubber mat flooring and a bare lightbulb fixture in the loft bedroom are part of the ADU's utilitarian appeal.

KIT OF PARTS

Prefabricated or modular homes are made in a factory and delivered to the site complete with finishes and fixtures. They tend to offer high quality and minimize construction time, but homeowners don't have the flexibility to design exactly what they want. Meanwhile, custom-designed homes can take a long time to construct, and their quality depends on the contractor. Panelized construction systems such as SIPs can offer the benefits of both: a panel manufacturing company translates an architect's plans for a custom structure into a set of panels, manufactures them, and sends them to the site for quick assembly.

For T+E+A+M's ADU, SIPs worked well and saved construction time. But the architects aren't stuck on them. "There is no magic solution or silver bullet," says Fure. "We've done a pretty close study of everything from modular construction to panelized products to stick building. The potential for savings depends on the project—the site, timeline, budget—so the best approach will vary."

The ADU has its own outdoor space, screened off from the rest of the backyard.

Extending back from the home's garage, the ADU is mostly hidden from the street. The ADU is not accessible from the garage; instead, you walk down a path next to the garage to reach the front entrance of the ADU.

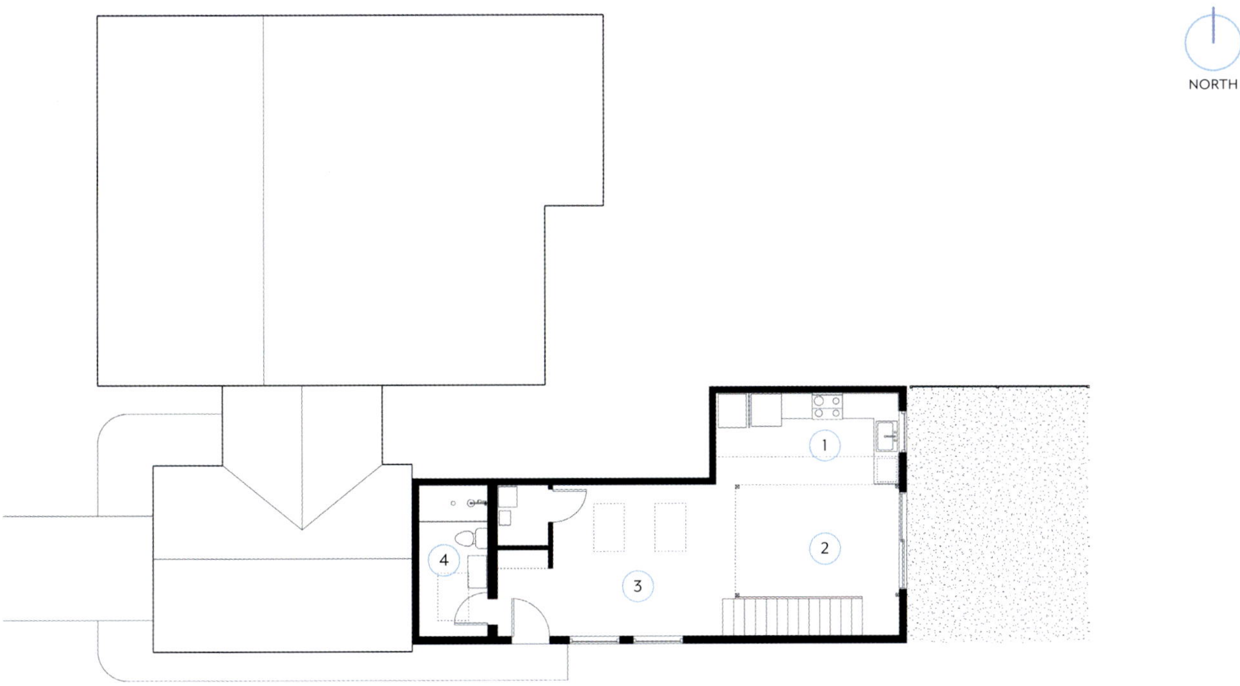

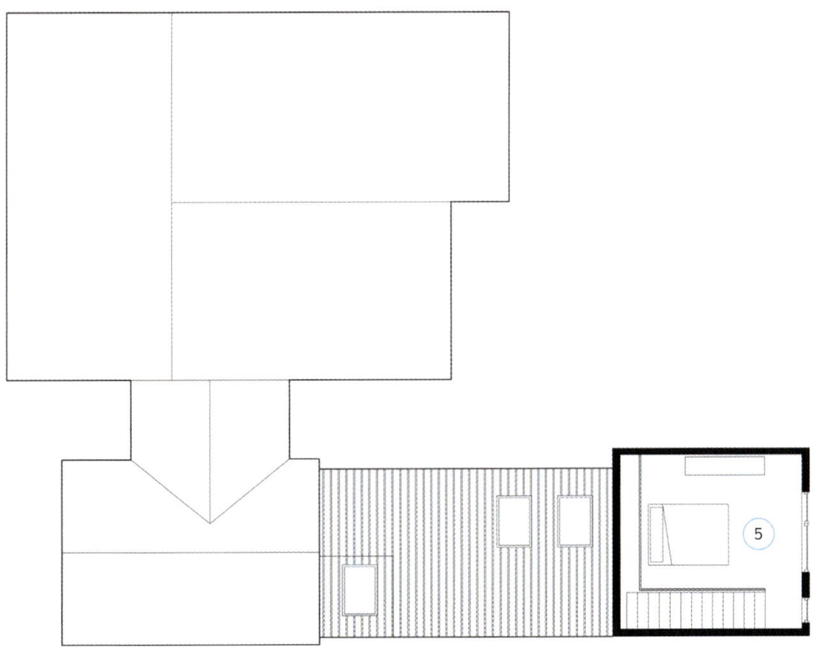

1. Kitchen
2. Dining
3. Living
4. Bath
5. Bedroom

BUDGET CHIC

A sculptural ceiling and bold colors add style to an ADU in Los Angeles.

PHOTOS COURTESY OF YOSHIHIRO MAKINO

Located on the east and west sides, skylights showcase the passage of the sun throughout the day, creating shifting patterns of light and color. The bright-yellow door to the main bedroom follows the contours of the stepped ceiling.

In the backyard of a house in L.A.'s Highland Park neighborhood, a modest tan-stuccoed house is the gateway into a colorful world that references the creativity of architects such as Luis Barragán and Gio Ponti. "We wanted to use all the tricks at our disposal to get the space to do more than what is expected, and so many of these artistic ideas are lost to the average American home," says architect Bo Sundius. "But we think the ADU can be a movement to rethink how we build and live."

Sundius and designer Hisako Ichiki, the cofounders of Bunch Design, have designed more than twenty ADUs, including two rental properties for themselves. After they built one at their home in Solano Canyon, they purchased a rental property in Highland Park, knowing that they could add an ADU there as well. Like many of their clients, their plan is to use the rent from the ADU to pay off the cost of construction in fifteen years; after that, the mortgage-free rent may come in handy for big life expenses. "We like doing these small but expansive projects in people's backyards—they really transform your opportunities as a homeowner," says Sundius.

Bunch Design gave the ADU a simple form and economical stucco finish. The recessed casement windows are standard off-the-shelf windows, without the typical thick trim—a nice way to get more design on a tight budget.

The living room opens to a private courtyard at the back of the property.

As a general philosophy, the two like to focus their design energy and budget on interiors. For their 880-square-foot ADU in Highland Park, which has two bedrooms and one bath, they wanted to create an interesting environment for their tenants. “People spend a lot of time in these small spaces, and we don’t want them to get cabin fever,” says Sundius. Influenced by the playful geometry of Gio Ponti’s work, they created an unusual exposed ceiling by switching the orientation of the roof joists. Normally, joints are placed perpendicular to the roof ridge; they placed them parallel with the ridge to produce a stepped ceiling. The space has an “Italian sense of fun,” says Sundius.

Ichiki and Sundius also admired architect Luis Barragán’s technique of placing boldly colored walls next to white plaster walls, so that the color would reflect off the white walls. They painted the top of the bathroom, which is a separate enclosure, an electric “Barragán pink”—light bounces off the “roof” of the room and lights up the main ceiling with a pink glow.

To make the ADU feel more spacious, the couple designed the walls so they don't continue all the way up to the ceiling, allowing light from skylights and clerestory windows to pass through the whole space. They thought about adding clear acrylic paneling for acoustic privacy, but none of their renters have asked for it so far. They did opt to put the toilet in its own completely enclosed room, while the bathtub and shower are in a separate room that has partial walls.

"The beautiful thing about drywall is that it's very sculptural," says Sundius. "It's boring if it's just white, but if you can get shadows and light to play on it, it can be quite dynamic."

Since the ADU would be rented out separately from the main residence, the architects oriented it toward the fence at the back. The city required a 5-foot setback, but they decided to increase the setback to 10 feet to create a private outdoor space for the ADU. "If you're living in the ADU, you don't want to have your barbecue in the backyard of the front house," says Sundius. "The ADU is a small single-family dwelling, so these are the nuances that you have to figure out."

The front door is accessed from the courtyard. Inspired by Barragán's fondness for knotty pine, the architects chose the inexpensive material for the flooring. The custom kitchen cabinetry was built by a local fabricator.

In the bathroom, a round acrylic skylight borrows light from the skylights in the roof above.

The shower and tub are in a separate room.

SPLITTING THE BATHROOM

Rather than combine all the functions together, the Bunch Design team created a split bathroom for the Highland Park ADU. The toilet is in one room, while the shower and tub are in another, and each has its own sink.

Common in Japan, where bathing is elevated to a ritual, the split bathroom also provides more flexibility. While a regular house might have a separate powder room for guests, splitting the bathroom provides a powder room within the limited square footage of an ADU. "We do like to separate the toilet from the bath when there is room, particularly in cases where the bathroom is accessible from the public space of the ADU," says Sundius.

The main bedroom has a back door to enable the ADU to function as a home office for the main house.

JANUS
GOD OF TIME

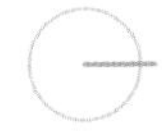

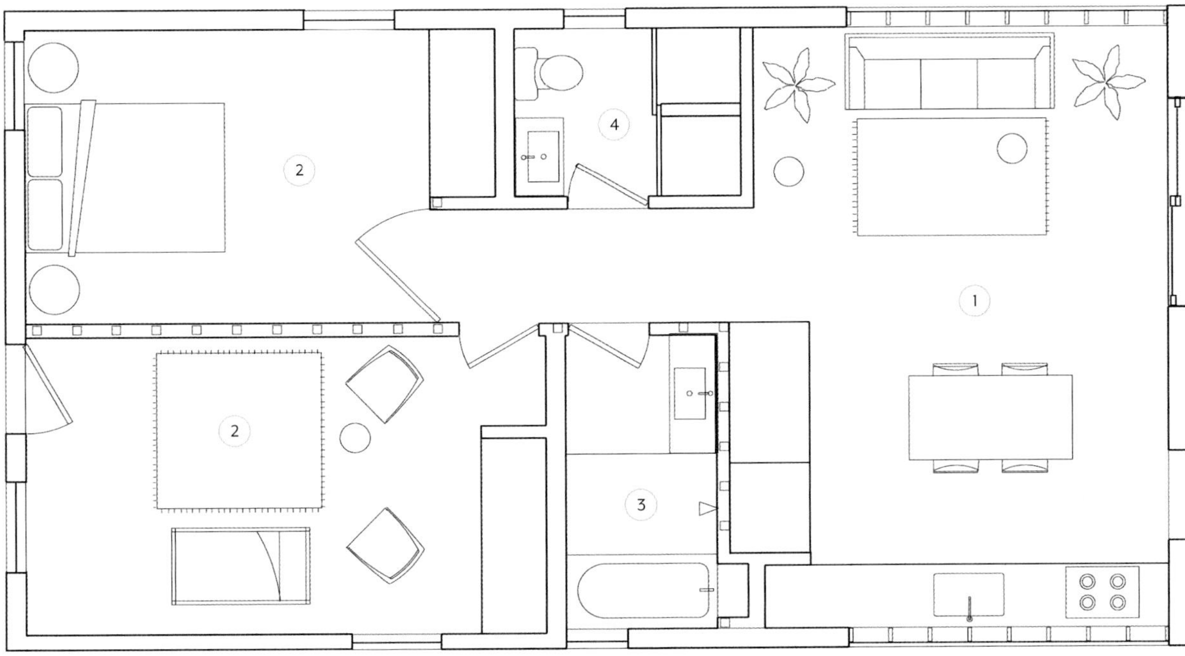

1. Dining/Living/Kitchen
2. Bedroom
3. Bathroom
4. WC/Laundry

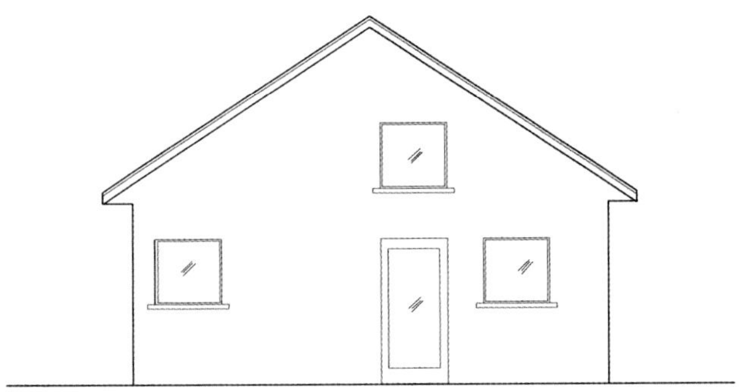

South Elevation

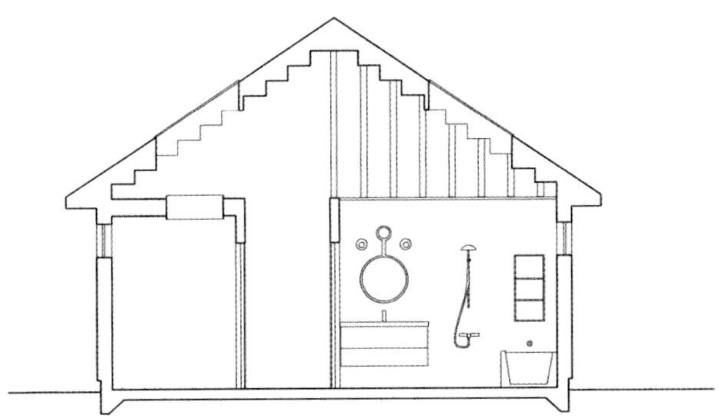

Section

The second bedroom can be used as a playroom or office.

BENDING THE RULES

Portland's ADU regulations result in an ADU with an unexpected shape.

EXTERIOR PHOTOS COURTESY OF SALLY SCHOOLMASTER; INTERIOR PHOTOS COURTESY OF DAVID PAPAZIAN

Although its shape is unconventional, the ADU's fiber-cement clapboard siding is traditional. The siding is painted a dark bronze, which Waechter likes because it is relatively easy to match with window cladding and light fixtures and complements a green garden.

Architect Ben Waechter wrestled with ADU height restrictions in Portland, Oregon, to meet his client's need for more space. The two-story ADU he designed technically follows the letter of the law but takes some creative liberties.

Ann, an interior designer, was living in a 1920s bungalow in inner southeast Portland. She asked Waechter to design an ADU in the back, intending to live in it and rent out the property in front. Her wish list included two bedrooms so she could have guests, and enough room for a large dining table to host dinners. And she wanted natural light. "I wanted it to feel open and have a lot of light, because it gets really gloomy and gray here in the winter, which is depressing," says Ann.

To conserve as much backyard as possible, Waechter envisioned a two-story structure. But at the time, ADUs could be a maximum of only 18 feet high, which essentially made it impossible to build a two-story ADU, since the floors would be too low.

However, the city measured the height of pitched roofs at the midpoint, not at the peak. So, Waechter got around the height limit by creating a much longer roof than the house needed. In this way, he was able to fit two bedrooms of comfortable proportions on the second floor while keeping the square footage to the maximum allowed amount of 800 square feet. The exaggerated roof, which measures 18 feet at its midpoint, created 10-foot-deep eaves, which the architect used to form sheltered porches on either side. The dramatic shape is modern but still feels familiar.

The downstairs level of the ADU is one large space, with two walls of glass that open to the side yards. The kitchen runs along the length of one wall, and the facing wall contains the stairwell, utilities, storage, and a small powder room. Upstairs, there are two bedrooms and a bathroom. According to Ann, she would have liked to have a little more space to install a bathtub, but everything else has turned out well.

Portland has revised its ADU regulations a couple of times since Ann's ADU was completed in 2015, increasing the maximum height to 20 feet. Waechter recently had a meeting with city planning and zoning staff, and one of the planners remembered his project. Says Waechter, "She said, 'Yeah, that's the project where we had to revisit all our rules.'"

The architect used the overscaled roof, which is 24 feet tall at its peak, to create covered patios on either side of the ADU. The deep eaves keep water well away from the foundation, so he was able to eliminate gutters and give the roofline a clean, sharp edge.

Glass walls on facing sides of the lower level fill the space with light.

There is no drywall on the lower level, except on the ceiling—maple plywood covers the kitchen cabinetry and built-in storage on the opposite wall.

HAPPY FEET

Using a concrete slab foundation as the flooring, as is the case in Ann's ADU, has several advantages. The concrete floor is incredibly durable, withstanding chipping and water damage. It also saves on cost since no additional flooring needs to be purchased and installed. During installation, it's possible to add small rocks, referred to as aggregate, to create visual interest or add a stain to change the color. As a final step, concrete floors are typically polished to create a more finished look.

One of the items on Ann's wish list was a concrete floor with radiant heating. "Radiant heat is quiet and not too dry and is more eco-friendly," says Ann. Installing a concrete slab foundation with radiant heating is an elegant solution. The hot-water pipes are embedded into the foundation, and concrete has a lot of thermal mass, so it retains heat and provides even warmth—a much more efficient way to heat a space than blowing hot air into a room.

GROUND FLOOR

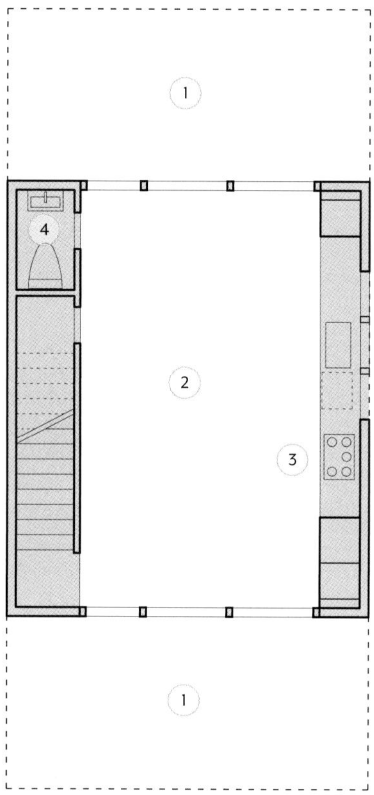

SECOND FLOOR

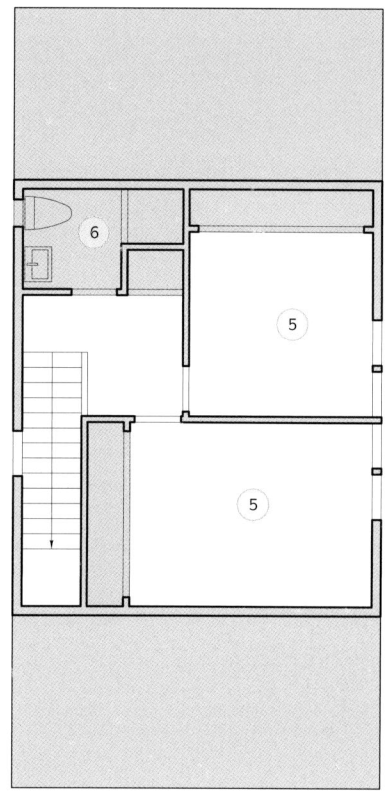

1. Patio
2. Living/Dining
3. Kitchen
4. Powder Room
5. Bedroom
6. Bathroom

SITE PLAN

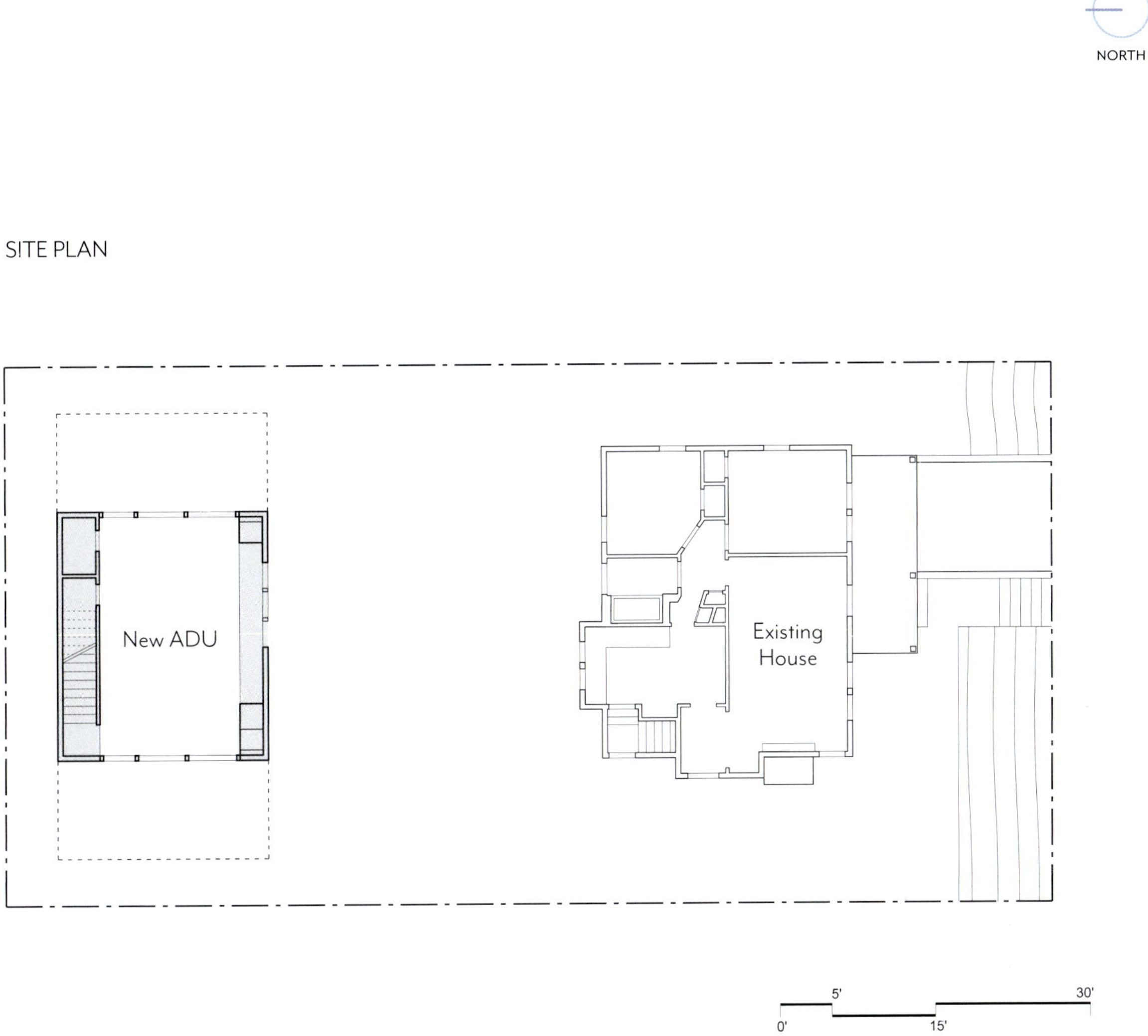

THE SKY'S THE LIMIT

A modest garage in L.A. becomes a fantasyland.

PHOTOS COURTESY OF MICHAEL WELLS

Architect Ben Warwas replaced the sloping driveway up to the garage with a raised deck to provide the ADU with valuable outdoor space.

Architect Ben Warwas of Byben made a deal with his client, a developer who came to him with a remodeling project. Warwas would renovate the small house in El Cerrito to get it ready for sale, but he would also have free rein to redesign its detached two-car garage into an ADU. "I hadn't designed an ADU yet at that point, and the agreement let me do whatever I wanted on a reasonable budget," says Warwas. "I was excited to do something interesting, given all the parameters."

Warwas, who worked for ten years as a contractor in between fashion school and architecture school, relished the challenge of designing the ADU on a low to moderate budget. He evaluated the garage and noted that its slab foundation and wood framing were in good condition, so converting it into an ADU didn't require expensive structural work.

The built-in linen closet at the end of the hallway has mirrored panels, fooling the eye into thinking that the space extends farther back. The white sculpture on the wall was created by Warwas out of wood.

The kitchen cabinetry was made by a local fabricator that uses CNC milling. "As long as you work within the limits of the machine, you can get a very custom kitchen without the cost," says Warwas. The upper cabinet doors are taller than the cabinets, allowing slivers of light from a hidden fixture to seep around the edges.

Making the one-bedroom, one-bathroom ADU feel bigger than its actual 400 square feet was the key challenge. Before embarking on this project, Warwas was skeptical that such a small dwelling could include a separate bedroom. To enlarge it, Warwas replaced the garage door with a sliding glass door and added a large deck so that the kitchen/living area flows through to the outdoor space. He used the plywood paneling on the kitchen cabinets to line the vaulted ceiling, so the cabinets appear to be part of one continuous surface. He also covered the hall linen closet with mirrored panels to create the illusion of more space. "There are moments in your peripheral vision when it doesn't feel tiny," he says.

The layout does give up a little space for more functionality. Warwas created a small hallway between the bedroom and the bathroom so that the bathroom could be a "public facility," as he puts it, instead of a private one that can be accessed only by walking through the bedroom. "This way, you can have a messy bedroom and still entertain guests," he observes.

The ADU owes much of its charm to its arched windows, which are inexpensive vinyl windows from a local window company. "Most windows are essentially made to order, so it's the material and the manufacturer that govern the price," points out Warwas. The ADU's signature cloud theme was a bit of an afterthought. He had already ordered the arched windows to make the facade more interesting, and only later envisioned them as part of a cloud. Unlike some other architects, Warwas relishes surface decoration. "Architects always view wallpaper as inferior to form," he says. "But I did my master's thesis in architecture school on how appliqué and form are equal."

The floor is covered in large-format ceramic tile, and the ceiling is finished with plywood panels.

Rather than mar ceilings with recessed can lights or ceiling-mounted fixtures, Warwas prefers to use sconces, pendants, and lamps.

A small arched window brings in natural light but is placed high for privacy.

From the other side of the retaining wall, there's a small hint of something special on the other side.

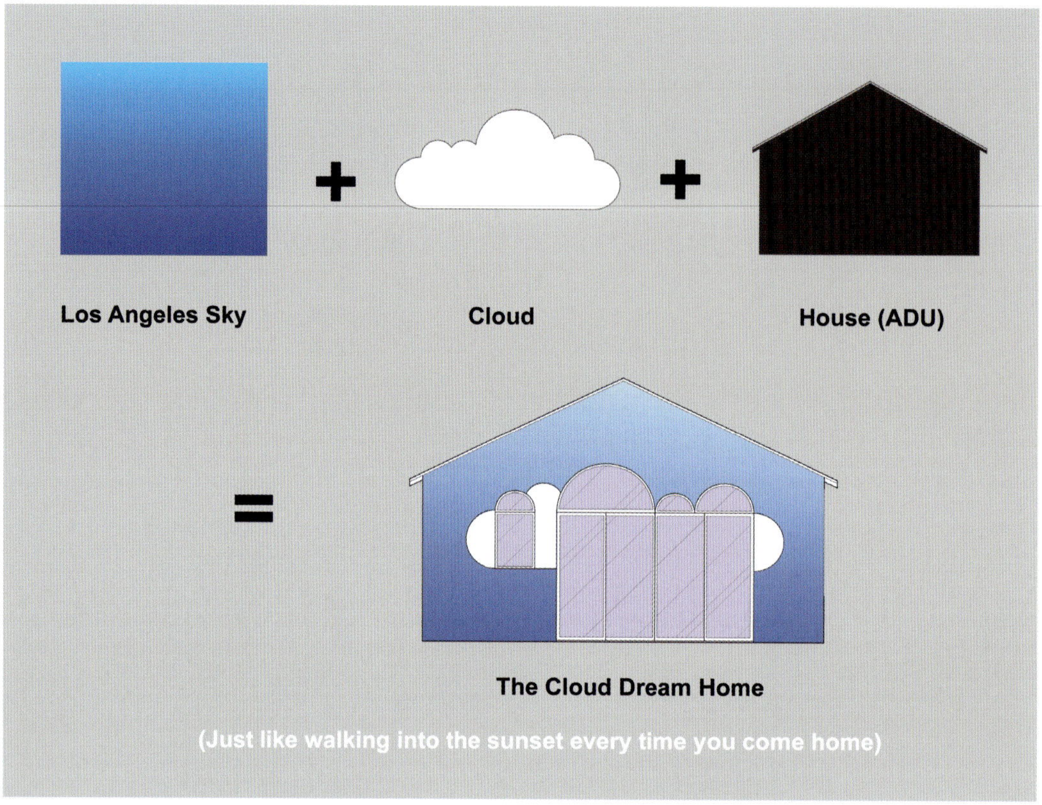

The architect's concept for transforming a modest garage

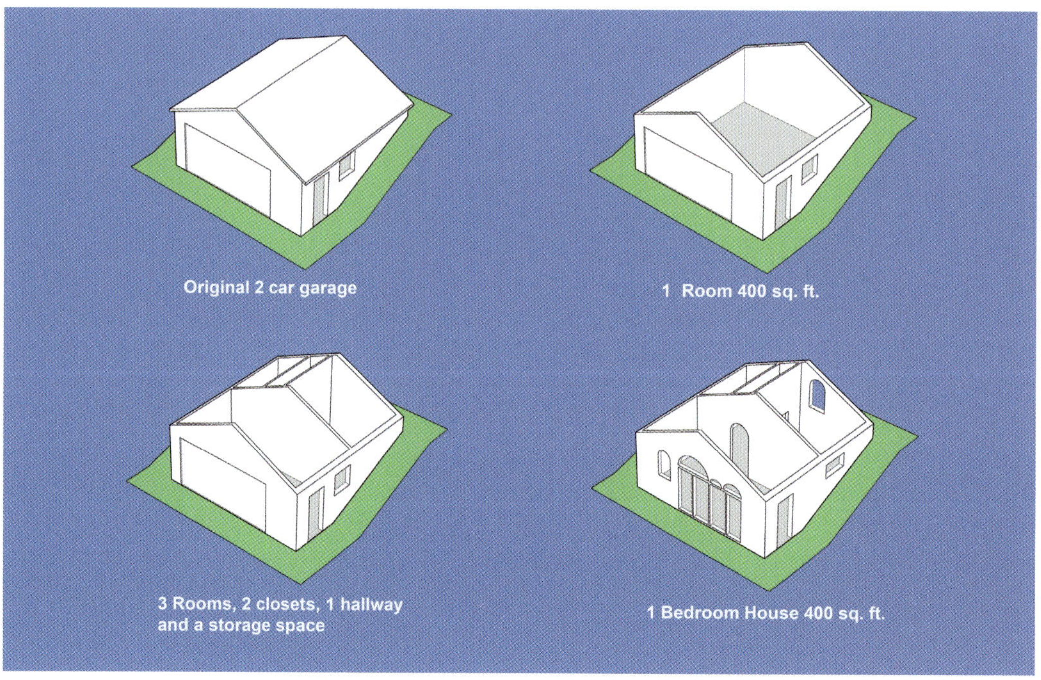

BEFORE: GARAGE

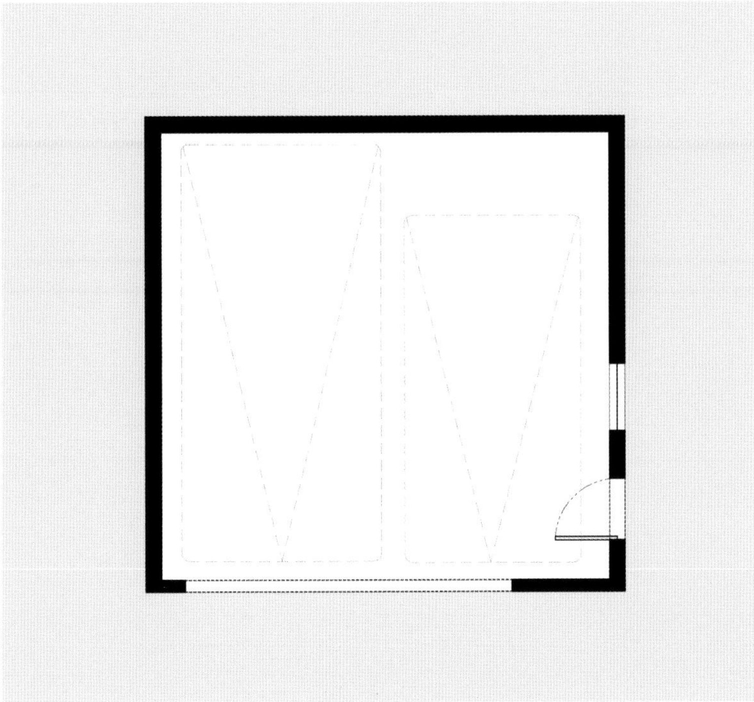

Original Two-Car Garage

AFTER: HOUSE

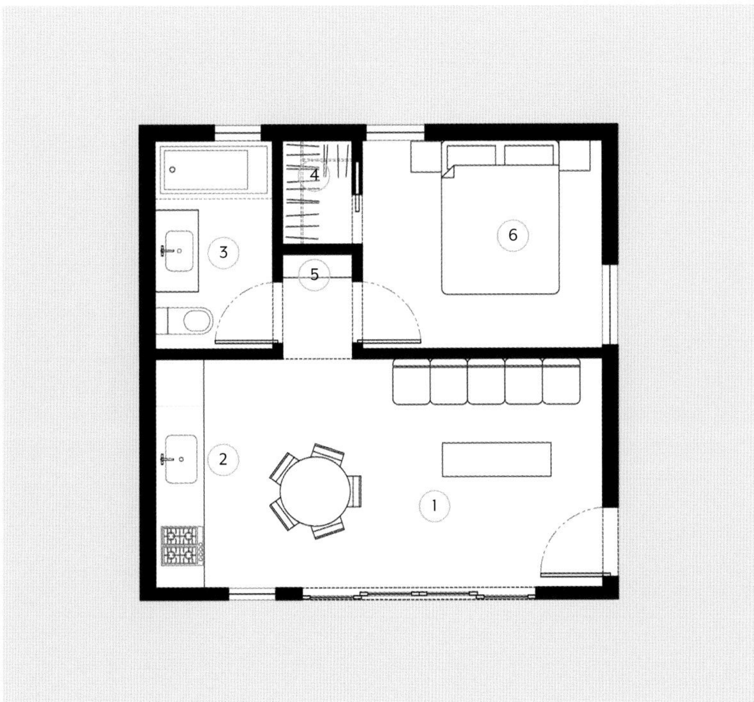

1. Living/Dining
2. Kitchen
3. Bathroom
4. Closet
5. Linen Closet
6. Bedroom

BUILD BACK BETTER

A catastrophic fire leads to a brand-new garage—and much more.

PHOTOS COURTESY OF ALYSSA LEE PHOTOGRAPHY

The interiors are bright with natural light, thanks to windows on all four sides and three skylights. Operable awning windows provide natural ventilation during the hot summers.

It was January 2018, and Kirsten and Michael had just watched the Minnesota Vikings lose the semifinal playoffs on TV when they heard the sound of breaking glass outside their Minneapolis home. Moments later, their garage was engulfed by a raging fire, caused by a defective extension cord. In the aftermath, they learned that the fire was so intense, even the concrete floor of the garage would have to be replaced. "Since we were going that far down, we decided to clean-sheet the project," says Michael, who works in computer security.

Architect Christopher Strom figured out how to design the ultimate garage for the couple. The new two-car garage has a one-bedroom ADU upstairs. While only 660 square feet, the dwelling includes an elevator. A key consideration in the design was accessibility: One of the couple's parents has Parkinson's, which affects the nervous system; hence the couple was planning for a time when an accessible space could come in handy. To combine a garage and an accessible ADU within the city's prescribed size limit of 1,300 square feet, Strom made some strategic choices. Given the amount of space taken up by the elevator, he moved the stairs outdoors, which "really unlocked some possibilities," he says. "Designing an ADU is a game of inches, not feet." While the bathroom isn't large enough for a wheelchair to turn around in, the zero-threshold shower has a bench and grab bars. Strom also located all the ADU's mechanical equipment in a closet within the garage, saving interior space upstairs.

To maximize interior space, architect Christopher Strom moved the stairs to the ADU outside, placing them at an angle to avoid blocking the door to the garage. The stairs are made with bar grating so they don't collect snow.

A covered landing at the top of the stairs doubles as a small deck, which is made of a composite material of recycled plastic and bamboo.

The ADU has an elevator for those who can't manage the stairs easily.

MIXSHAKESTIR

The cabinetry is from IKEA and has custom doors. By extending the kitchen countertop all the way to the window frames, rather than stopping at a sill, the architect created more usable counter space.

Whenever possible, Strom likes to wrap windows in ADUs around corners to provide a panoramic view and increase the sense of space.

The compact space feels spacious, which is a testament both to the architect and the homeowners, who handled the interior design. "I binged-watched *Tiny House Nation* to get ideas, like installing a wall-mounted faucet in the bathroom to have more counter space," says Kirsten, a consultant on agriculture and climate change. To make the ADU feel expansive, light comes in from all four sides as well as through skylights. Automated shades and operable windows help the ADU stay cool during the hot summers.

The ADU is also designed for comfort during Minnesota's intensely cold winters. It has heavy insulation and a tight building envelope. In addition to hydronic radiant floor heating, it also has an electric mini-split system for heating and cooling (the mini-split warms up the space quickly, while the radiant floor system

needs time to kick in). It also generates enough electricity through its rooftop solar panels to power itself as well as handle a portion of the main house's energy needs.

From the time it was completed in 2020, the ADU has served a wide range of purposes. In addition to hosting houseguests, including some who relied on the elevator, it was a getaway for the family during the pandemic. It continues to serve as a peaceful retreat for Kirsten's meditation sessions. "It's nice to be in a different space that isn't filled with all our stuff," says Kirsten. "One of our friends joked that we built our vacation cabin in our own backyard," says Michael.

To maximize space, the vanity, faucet, and toilet all are wall mounted. A makeup mirror is a thoughtful feature that gives the bathroom a hotel-like feel.

The shower is designed with no threshold, a bench, and grab bars for older guests (and aging in place). All the doors have levers instead of knobs.

A bird's-eye view of the ADU shows how it fits into the existing neighborhood.

To make the ADU more visually prominent than the garage, Strom dropped the forest-green corrugated-steel cladding so that it aligns with the top of the garage door. The rooftop solar panels were placed strategically to allow room for skylights.

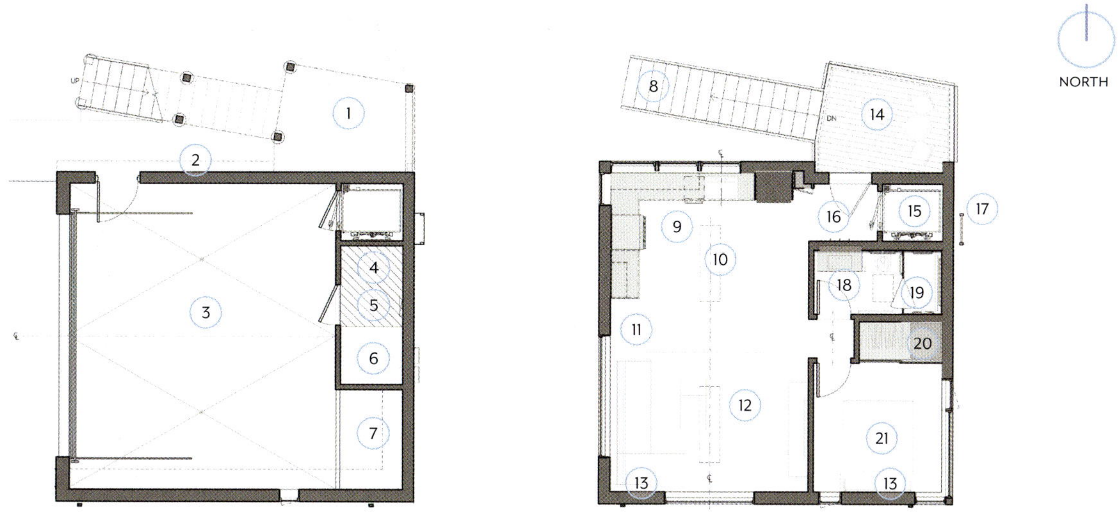

1. Deck Above
2. Cantilevered Kitchen Above
3. Garage
4. Mechanical
5. H.R.V.
6. Combination Boiler/Forced-Air Unit
7. In-Floor Heating
8. Open Bar Grating
9. Kitchen/Dining
10. 3 Skylights
11. In-Floor Heating
12. Living Room
13. Mini-Splits
14. Entry Deck
15. Elevator
16. Entry
17. Roof Ladder for Solar Panels
18. Bathroom
19. Shower
20. Washer/Dryer
21. Bedroom

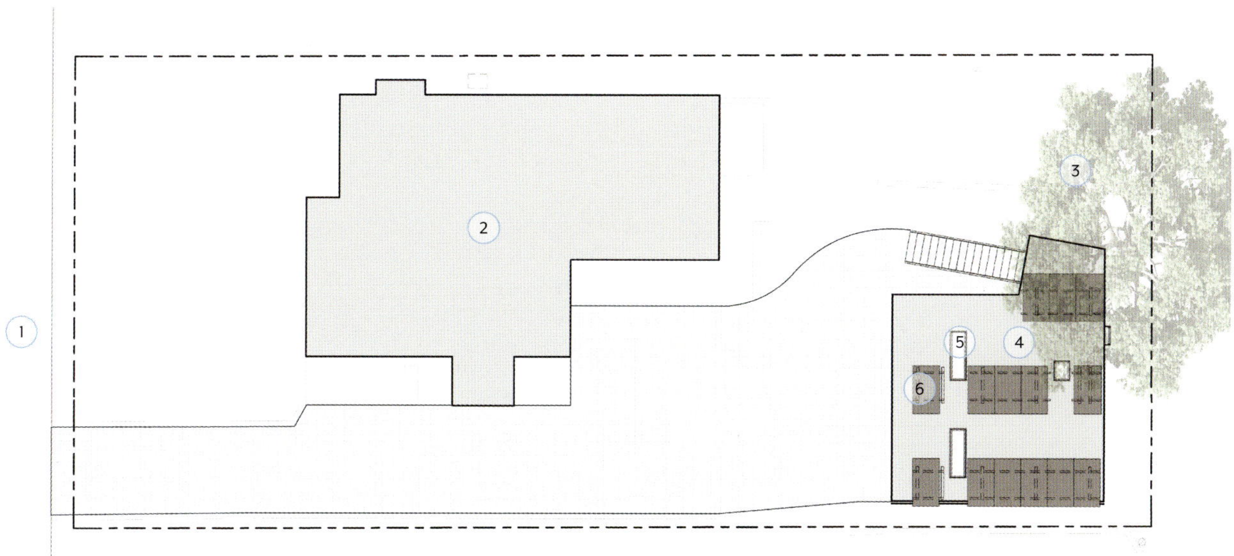

SITE PLAN
1. Street
2. Existing Primary Residence
3. Preserved Tree
4. ADU
5. Skylights
6. Solar Panels

MOVING ON UP

A young family buys an unusually long lot in Silicon Valley to build upward.

PHOTOS COURTESY OF CORTEZ MEDIA GROUP

Architect Adam Mayberry accentuated the 8-foot-tall front door by painting it bright yellow. For the stucco-clad volume, he created a roof overhang with exposed joists, tapering the joist ends for a more refined appearance.

Leonardo and Jennifer, who had been living in a small house in the Silicon Valley city of San Jose, were running out of space. They had a young daughter but anticipated having another child and wanted to be able to host their parents as well. Fortunately, they found a 1924 Craftsman in the city's Rose Garden neighborhood on a property that had a lot of potential—a skinny but 200-foot-deep lot. "It was a ridiculously long lot, too long to go to waste," says Leonardo. "We thought, 'This could be our "forever home." Let's just keep adding to it.'"

After the couple moved in and completed an unfinished addition, they began contemplating an ADU where their parents could stay. At the time, Leonardo, a design executive, was working for Facebook, and celebrated architect Frank Gehry was designing its new offices. The open workspace emphasized raw industrial materials and had a main stair clad in plywood. "I'm a huge fan of Frank Gehry, and the 'unfinished' finished look is integral to Facebook's culture—it's a hacker company, so nothing is ever close to being done," says Leonardo. One of Leonardo's tasks was to choose artists to create installations within the new Gehry building; he had a vision of filling their ADU with art and design as well.

The kitchen cabinetry is from IKEA.

The plywood-clad staircase complements the concrete flooring, which has a dark stain that was added at the time the foundation was poured.

GOOD DESIGN IS INNOVATIVE
HACK
San FRANCISCO

Architect Adam Mayberry of Mayberry Workshop, who has designed about forty ADUs, collaborated with his clients to create a two-story, two-bedroom ADU. They were limited to 900 square feet, the maximum area allowed by the city at the time. "We wanted it to feel like a lot of space, and the only way to do that was to go with vaulted ceilings and have one room upstairs," says Leonardo.

The ADU has two halves: a two-story volume containing the bedrooms, and another volume that holds the great room and is almost double height. Both parts have pitched ceilings to create more-dynamic spaces and are connected by a sculptural staircase clad in marine-grade plywood. "The state of California dictates minimum heights for one- and two-story ADUs, which I think is a good idea because an ADU is a home, not a second-class structure,"

The ADU's main gathering area has relatively few windows to provide more wall space for art. An area under the stairs is used for a cozy office nook.

says Mayberry. Breaking the ADU up into two volumes—one covered in corrugated-metal siding, the other clad in stucco—reduces the scale of the whole building and makes it more backyard-friendly. "The metal siding isn't more expensive than stucco and lets us bridge the gap between traditional suburban homes and a more urban aesthetic," notes Mayberry.

When health problems kept the in-laws from moving in full-time, Leonardo and Jennifer initially offered it as a long-term rental. Today, family and friends stay there when they visit, and the couple also lists it as a home share. And occasionally Jennifer, who is a stay-at-home mom to their two young kids, goes there for a staycation where she is free from domestic obligations. "We all need to escape sometimes," says Leonardo.

The whole stair is clad in plywood.

The upstairs bedroom has a vaulted ceiling.

In the upstairs bedroom, a reading nook faces the window. In the alcove next to the chair, there is a bookcase just out of sight.

DESIGNING WITH PLYWOOD

Architects such as Frank Gehry are fond of plywood for its industrial simplicity. The material offers the warmth of wood on a budget and is easily sourced. "Installing plywood requires greater attention to detail and has a higher cost than drywall but is a great way to add warmth and texture to a space," says architect Rebecca Marsh of SHED Architecture & Design.

The staircase in Leonardo and Jennifer's home is clad in 3/4-inch-thick plywood. In other projects in this book, plywood is used as a wall finish. The plywood can be applied over drywall, which makes it easier to install precisely. Or it can be used in lieu of drywall and installed directly on top of wall framing with the addition of a vapor barrier.

As a wall finish, architects recommend using marine-grade plywood, which is the highest grade of plywood and has the fewest knots and the smoothest surface. "If you're contemplating plywood, consider how much grain or movement you want to see in the paneling, and what color tone you are looking for," says Marsh. "Some species, like fir, have a warmer tone, while pine and Baltic birch have cooler tones." After installation, a clear coat of polyurethane is added to protect the surface and make it stain resistant. It's another reason to like plywood—unlike drywall, it doesn't need to be regularly repainted to look good.

The ground-level bedroom looks out on a lushly landscaped yard.

A wall-mounted toilet saves space in the bathroom.

SITE PLAN

1. ADU
2. Existing Garage
3. Existing Dwelling

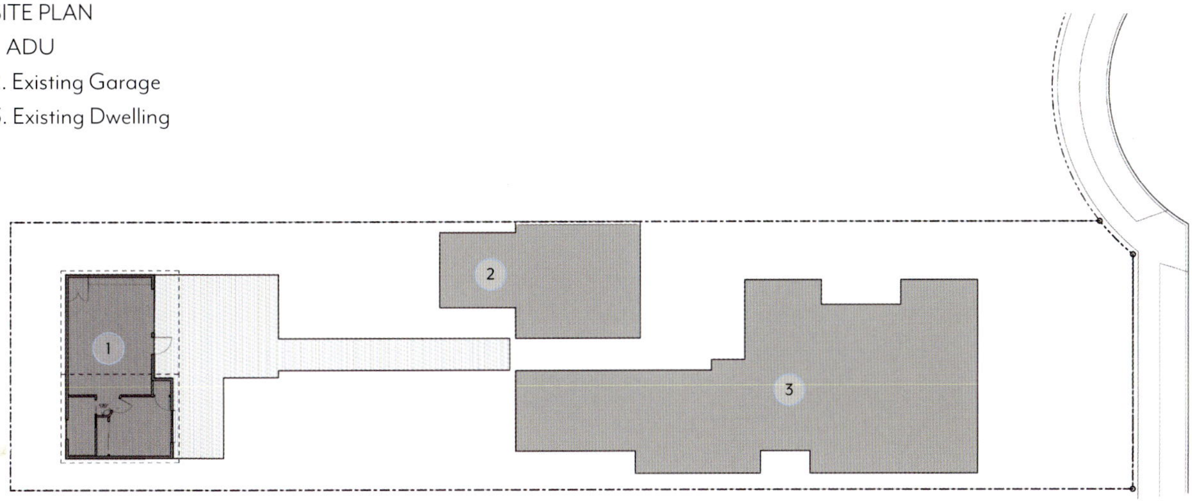

SECOND FLOOR

1. Open to Below
2. Closet
3. Bedroom

GROUND FLOOR

4. Washer/Dryer
5. Dishwasher
6. Kitchen
7. Dining
8. Living Room
9. Closet
10. Bath
11. Closet
12. Bedroom

DIRECTORY

Abodu
Redwood City, California
www.abodu.com
www.facebook.com/MyAbodu
Instagram: @myabodu
Pinterest: @myabodu

Bunch Design
Los Angeles, California
www.bunchdesign.net
www.facebook.com/bunchdesignla
Instagram: @bunch_design
Pinterest: @buncharch

Byben
Los Angeles, California
https://byben.com
Instagram: @ben_warwas

Christopher Strom Architects
Minneapolis, Minnesota
https://christopherstrom.com
www.facebook.com/christopherstromarchitects
Instagram: @christopherstromarchitects
Pinterest: @christopherstromarchitects

Davey McEathron Architecture
Austin, Texas
www.daveymarchitecture.com
Instagram: @davey.mceathron.architecture

Design, Bitches
Los Angeles, California
https://designbitches.com
www.facebook.com/profile.php?id=100064339540200
Instagram: @design_bitches
Pinterest: @designbitches

IwamotoScott Architecture
San Francisco, California
www.iwamotoscott.com
www.facebook.com/IwamotoScott
Instagram: @iwamotoscott
Pinterest: @iwamotoscott
www.linkedin.com/company/iwamotoscott-architecture

MA+HG Architects
Vancouver, British Columbia
https://mahg.ca
Instagram: @mahgarchitects

Mayberry Workshop
San Jose, California
www.mayberryworkshop.com
www.facebook.com/MayberryWorkshop
Instagram: @mayberryworkshop

Mork-Ulnes Architects
San Francisco, California, and Oslo, Norway
www.morkulnes.com
www.facebook.com/morkulnesarchitects
Instagram: @morkulnesarchitects

ORA
Los Angeles, California
www.ora.la
www.facebook.com/ora.la.arch
Instagram: @ora.la_arch
www.linkedin.com/company/ora-architecture-design

SHED Architecture & Design
Seattle, Washington
www.shedbuilt.com
www.facebook.com/SHEDSeattle
Instagram: @shedarchitecture

Side Angle Side
Austin, Texas
www.sideangleside.co
Instagram: @sideangleside.co

T+E+A+M
Ann Arbor, Michigan
https://tpluseplusaplusm.us
Instagram: @tpluseplusaplusm

Waechter Architecture
Portland, Oregon
https://waechterarchitecture.com
www.facebook.com/waechterarchitecture
Instagram: @waechter_architecture

INDEX

Lydia Lee is a frequent contributor to leading architecture and design publications and is based in the San Francisco Bay Area. Her award-winning writing focuses on design that reduces our carbon footprint and was honored with a 2022 award for architectural criticism from the Los Angeles Press Club. She is a passionate advocate for more bike lanes and more housing. You can find her on Instagram (@lydiawlee) and at Lydialee.com.